GET RICH ON OTHER PEOPLE'S MONEY

William H. Pivar

ARCO PUBLISHING, INC.
NEW YORK

Published by Arco Publishing, Inc.
219 Park Avenue South, New York, N.Y. 10003

Library of Congress Cataloging in Publication Data

Pivar, William H.
    Get rich on other people's money.

    1. Real estate investment.   I. Title.
HD1382.5.P58   332.63'24   81–2019
ISBN 0–668–05144–2 (Cloth Edition) AACR2
ISBN 0–668–05152–3 (Paper Edition)

Printed in the United States of America

Contents

Contents

Contents

Careful Action—Contingency Clauses—Assuming
Assessments—Income Property—Assuming Loans—
Abstracts and Title Insurance—Balloon Payments,
Refinancing and Foreclosure—Is Personal Property
Included in the Sale?—Seller or Buyer Responsibility?—
Rent Arrearages—Taking Title—Liquidated
Damages—Confirming a Serious Offer—Release
Clauses and Blanket Encumbrances—Acceptance of
Offers

Contents

Contents

Property is desirable, is a positive good in the world. Let not him who is houseless pull down the house of another, but let him work diligently and build one for himself, thus by example assuring that his own shall be safe from violence when built.

—*Abraham Lincoln, 1864*

1

Why Real Estate?

For hundreds of years the only true wealth was considered to be real estate. Without real estate ownership a person was considered a second-class citizen; in fact, in many countries ownership was reserved for a favored few. Our country was founded by immigrants who were motivated by the desire to own land; a free land to many meant freedom to own property. Even today many people consider real estate to be the foundation for all riches.

More millionaires have achieved their wealth through real estate than from all other endeavors combined. The progressive income tax, which takes more as you earn more, has eliminated most other paths to riches. With our current economy, even with both husband and wife working and earning good salaries, most families find it impossible to accumulate much wealth.

TAXES AS AN ENCOURAGEMENT TO REAL ESTATE INVESTMENT

Our tax laws, while harsh on earnings, actually encourage ownership of real estate. Interest and property tax payments are always deductible expenses. Therefore, a person buying a home can afford to make a significantly higher payment for a home purchase than could be paid for a non-deductible rent payment. As an example, suppose you could buy a property with $800 per month payments or rent a similar property for $600 per month. Of the $800 payment probably $750 will apply to interest and taxes. An adjusted gross income in excess of $20,200. for a couple filing a joint return would place any additional earnings in a 24 percent federal tax bracket. If you add to this figure the applicable state income taxes, this hypothetical couple would probably be in at least a 33⅓ percent tax bracket. In the case above this would result in a

$250 per month savings through lower tax liability, or (one third of $750) a true out-of-pocket cost of ownership of $550 per month. Since the rental payment of $600 is not deductible in the example given, home ownership with monthly payments of $800 per month would actually be $50 per month less expensive than paying rent of $600.

Savings accounts are being eroded by inflation. Even with the interest earned, many people have seen their savings shrink in terms of purchasing power. A person earning 12 percent during a period of 15 percent inflation is going to be a poorer person at the end of the year.

INFLATION

Real estate is considered an inflationary hedge because values have increased at even a greater rate than has inflation. Unlike gold or stocks and bonds, which fluctuate in value with every newspaper headline, real estate values have in most instances been on an upward climb since World War II.

Of course, the inflationary increases in construction labor and material costs have resulted in higher costs, but there are other factors that have increased real estate values. The market force of supply and demand has pushed prices up. The post World War II baby boom is moving through the age cycles. These people are now setting up new households. Within a few years they will be a dominant factor in the second home market. We have also seen a sociological change with the growth of single-person and single-parent households. The increase in number of households, not necessarily population increases, results in demand increases. You should remember that no one is making any more land. The supply and demand law of the market place dictates that even without inflation, increases in demand from qualified buyers must result in higher prices.

We are seeing more and more people who desire to protect their savings turn to real estate. Also, the United States has recently been discovered by foreign investors who consider our real estate prices bargains compared to European or Asian values. This increased demand means even higher prices.

The greater part of the net worth of average homeowners is the equity in their homes. This has been caused by the great appreciation in value which homes have had over the past decade. Housing for a homebuyer today is more than shelter. It is an investment. Second homes are not looked at as luxuries anymore; they are just good, additional investments. During inflationary times buyers should consider buying the finest home they can afford. As inflation continues, not only will the high payments become reasonable or low, but the homeowner will benefit by greater appreciation. Inflation does not have to rob you. You can use inflation to help meet your goals of financial security.

ADVANTAGES TO OWNING REAL PROPERTY

One mistake many people make is waiting for interest rates to drop. While they wait, prices rise and the interest rate still might not come down. Even if you paid no income tax, you will be ahead if the rate of interest you pay for a real estate investment is less than the annual rate of increase in real estate values. We have seen very few years in which property values have failed to increase at a greater rate than the interest rates charged for real estate loans. If you pay income tax, then the advantage in owning real property is much greater. Assume you are in the 40 percent tax bracket (total of federal and state income tax) for your top dollar of income. If you are paying 15 percent interest on a loan, it only costs you 9 percent. Since the interest is deductible, Uncle Sam really pays the other 6 percent for you. With double digit inflation an average investment should increase in value at a rate far in excess of 9 percent each year.

Even though temporary unavailability of financing or the high cost of borrowing money may cause a temporary leveling off of values and in some cases a temporary drop in value, we can expect that inflation coupled with increased demand will keep our real estate market rising. You will see that inflation is not a prerequisite to making money in real estate, but it can help.

In addition to inflation, growing concern for the environment has led to much greater development costs and time delays for required approvals. This has contributed to the increased costs for new housing, which in turn tends to raise the value of existing housing.

SAFETY IN REAL ESTATE

Real estate has proved to be one of the safest investments possible. While there is some element of risk to every investment, the risk in real estate is minimal when compared with stock market investments. Over half of the new businesses which open each year don't last one year and few last as long as five years. The safety of real estate investments, compared with business investments, is reflected in a foreclosure rate far less than 1 percent. Real estate foreclosures have been rare in the last thirty years.

A major advantage of real estate is leverage. Unlike other investors, real estate investors seldom use all their own money. By buying with a low downpayment or even no downpayment and obtaining financing, they use other people's money to make money. As an example, suppose you purchased a lot for $10,000 and paid all cash. If the lot were to increase in value 10 percent you would have made a $1,000 profit, which would be a 10 percent profit on your investment. If, however, you had purchased the same lot with only a $1,000 downpayment, your $1,000 profit would now be a 100 percent profit on your investment. Financing real estate is the easiest way to find others to help you attain financial security.

Your monthly payment will actually decrease each month for real estate investments. As inflation continues, you will be making payments with ever cheaper dollars. The person who is most in debt therefore benefits the most. As an example, if a person had $100,000 to invest and purchased a six-unit building for $200,000, that person would get some benefit from inflation but nowhere near the benefit obtainable by buying a twenty-four-unit apartment building for $700,000 and financing $600,000 of the purchase price.

YOU CAN GET RICH

If your desire is to be a millionaire, you can achieve your goal by going into debt and letting inflation help you. If you can purchase real estate on which you owe $2,000,000 and can hold on to it for five years, you will be a millionaire. With only a 10 percent inflation (and we can expect that real estate values will increase at least that much), within five years your equity for average purchases should give you your million dollar equity. And that is without even compounding the inflation. In actual practice the inflation rate applies to the increased value, not the original cost. If you make careful selections of property, you should be able to do even better than average increases. It may sound too simple to be true, but it is the formula which has turned thousands of people into millionaires. This book will show you many different ways to obtain real estate with no or low downpayments. You will find that it doesn't necessarily take money to make money in real estate.

You may have heard the term *pyramiding* in connection with real estate. There is nothing mystical about it. Pyramiding is simply the trading or reinvestment of your equity into more or larger properties as inflation increases your equity.

Depreciation for Tax Purposes.   Besides appreciating in value, improved real property can be depreciated for tax purposes. Depreciation shelters other income from taxes. Suppose you have an income property which provides $10,000 per year in actual income. Now assume your expenses are $9,000, so the property provides you with $1,000 in profit. If the building itself cost $100,000 and had a life expectancy of twenty-five years, you could depreciate the building at least 4 percent each year, or $4,000. Depreciation is treated as an expense for tax purposes even though there is no out-of-pocket money spent. It is a paper deduction only. For tax purposes you would now show a total of $13,000 in expenses and only $10,000 in income. It means that you have a loss on the property of $3,000. You can cover this loss with $3,000 of your other income which is thereby sheltered from income taxes. The $1,000 you have received in cash is also sheltered from income taxes. If a person were in the 50 percent tax bracket (federal and state), it would take $8,000 in income to net the $4,000 that was sheltered by the depreciation. While a tax shelter might not appear meaningful if you currently are in a low tax bracket, as your income increases so will the importance of the benefits obtainable by depreciation.

Negative Cash Flow. Some investors find that even property with a negative cash flow is desirable. Even though a property operates at a loss, the net effect of the loss can be overcome by depreciation. In the 50 percent tax bracket a $5,000 cash loss is overcome by $10,000 in depreciation. If the depreciation is greater than $10,000, then the net effect to the owner will be positive.

Long-Term Capital Gains. A major advantage of real estate as an investment is that profit on sales of property held over one year is taxed as a long-term capital gain. What this means is that you have to pay only 40 percent of the taxes which would be paid for the same amount of money taken as wages. Under capital gains, 60 percent of the gain is exempt from taxation.

REAL ESTATE INVESTMENTS CAN BUY THEMSELVES

If you can buy a property where the income is sufficient to make the payments, then the property buys itself. If you could buy a $250,000 building with $20,000 down with a twenty-year loan and your income from the building makes the payments, in twenty years the building will be paid for. You will have turned $20,000 into $250,000, and there is nothing magical about it. In addition, inflation should have increased the building's value at least several times, so that instead of a $250,000 building you very well might have one worth $1,000,000. While spendable income is nice to have, income normally will not make you rich. Appreciation in value is what makes real estate investors wealthy.

The amount of your loan payment which applies to your loan principal may seem to be a cash expense, but it is really increasing your equity in the property by reducing the loan. This is a phantom income because you don't actually see it in your pocketbook. Nevertheless, it is a positive element of ownership. This phantom income will be realized when the property is sold.

Inflation Increases Income. As inflation increases, income also increases. If you have a fixed mortgage payment, the increase in income will turn a negative cash flow into a positive cash flow. Such a property would also offer the investor the advantages of depreciation to shelter income and appreciation for eventual profit.

Pride in Ownership.   There is another advantage of real estate. This is an intangible value upon which no price can be set. It is the psychological income you receive from owning property. Feelings of self-pride, security and confidence accompany ownership. Many people have found that property ownership has filled their need for a sense of belonging and having a place in life.

Advantages in Illiquid Investments.   Real estate, once purchased, protects the timid owner. While an owner of stocks can sell them in a matter of minutes, real estate is an illiquid investment. This means that it cannot readily be converted to cash. A momentary scare or whim will seldom result in a sale which will later be regretted.

While real estate may be an illiquid investment, it is possible to pump money out of a real estate investment in a relatively short time. This can be accomplished by using the property as security for a loan or increasing an existing loan by refinancing.

MAKING YOUR OWN DECISION

Every fifty-year-old wishes he or she had invested in real estate twenty years earlier. In fact, as a young boy, I remember my grandfather lamenting that the days of big profits in real estate were over. He, of course, was wrong, and you are also if you think as he did. The parade hasn't passed you by.

Many people who watched property increase from $100 an acre to $1,000 or more won't buy now even though the present price may very well be a bargain compared to what is likely to happen in the future. These people look to the past and refuse to look ahead. There are still excellent opportunities today. Don't look back at today and utter those three sad words, *I could have . . .*

Age is not a factor in real estate investment. Some investors who retired with modest incomes have become millionaires during their retirement years. At the other extreme I know of a college freshman who started out with $2,000. He invested in a run-down rooming house and was a millionaire before he finished graduate school.

Your decision to invest in real estate should be your own, but it should be made only after careful consideration. Don't ask friends or relatives what to do if they are not investing themselves. They won't tell you to do something they are too timid to do themselves. In addition many people feel that advice not to do something is the safest advice to give. You can't win in real estate until you get into the game, and you're not in the game until you commit yourself to buy.

Real estate has given me financial security. It allowed me to walk away from a high-paying position which I disliked intensely. I am able to do my own thing, which is teaching real estate at a community college near Palm Springs, California, in the winter and fishing in Wisconsin during the summer.

You can do the same. Many of my students have followed my advice to independence. I will tell you what you need to know, but you must do it by yourself.

The first man to fence in a piece of land saying, "This is Mine . . ." was the real founder of civil society.

—Jean-Jacques Rousseau, 1754

2

Investment Alternatives

BUYING SINGLE-FAMILY HOMES

For many years the "experts" advised people not to invest in single-family homes, saying they provided a poor return on the investment. Those who failed to heed this advice prospered.

When you measure income against price paid for a single-family home, it does appear as a poor investment; however, income is not the criterion to use. The criterion is appreciation. Since World War II the appreciation of single family homes has been phenomenal. As long as our government fails to control inflation (and control does not appear imminent), we can expect values to continue to rise.

Financing. A major advantage offered by single-family homes is financing. You can obtain a higher loan-to-value ratio for single-family homes than for any other investment. In many instances, such as Veterans Administration (VA) financing and some low-income Federal Housing Administration (FHA) loans, owner-occupied homes can be purchased without any cash downpayment.

A disadvantage of single-family homes as investments is that rarely will the rent make the debt payments unless a very substantial downpayment is made. However, as inflation continues, increased rents after a few years will often result in a turn-around and a positive cash flow.

While real estate is generally considered an illiquid investment, not readily converted to cash, single-family homes are the most liquid of real estate investments. Generally they can be sold in a far shorter time than other real estate and home equity can be readily used as collateral for loans. A single-family home is also the most readily rentable of the real estate investments. The sheer abundance of homes is an advantage to an investor.

8

There are usually plenty of homes on the market offered at a wide variety of prices and terms.

BUILDING HOMES FOR RESALE

Shortly after I graduated from college, I built my first home for resale. I found an inexpensive lot, a small builder who gave me a good price and a bank which gave me an excellent construction loan. My total cash assets at the time were around $500. Luckily, I sold the house for a profit before it was completed.

I say luckily because I had made some serious mistakes. I had looked for the cheapest lot. In terms of resale the cheapest lot is usually the most expensive lot. You should look for a lot in a better area because location sells. It has often been said that the three most important considerations in buying real estate are location, location and location.

In addition to a poor location, I picked a very contemporary plan. You know, one of those ugly homes with sharp angles which you see featured in the magazine sections of the Sunday newspapers but which few people build. This type of house is usually difficult to sell although everyone wants to see it. Homes which are radically different normally have limited markets. If you wish to build a house for resale, choose something that more people will purchase, such as a Colonial, Cape Cod, Spanish or standard Ranch design. Many builders have found it can be fatal to be overly innovative in home design unless the house is presold.

Building for Owner Occupancy. There are a number of investors who either build or have a home built for them. The investor moves in until the house can be sold and then builds another. This is a very low-risk way to operate and can be very profitable. A disadvantage is that the investor may begin to feel like a gypsy.

In my neighborhood we have a young couple with children who live in the houses they build. Both former real estate students of mine, the wife is an accomplished designer who designs all their homes. They build each home as their own, obtaining excellent financing. They have fabulous furniture, which makes the house look very good for resale purposes. When one house is sold, the couple starts building the next one. At times they have had to store their furniture and rent a furnished home for several months.

This couple has now expanded to the point where they build several homes at one time. I have been told that they now build with cash so that they have no loan payments to make. They currently live in a house which is on the market for over $500,000. This is pretty good for a couple who started out with salaried jobs and little savings just ten years ago.

Although this couple act as their own general contractors and hire subcontractors for all the work, some people give the entire job to a general contractor. Still others will physically build each house themselves. An advantage of building homes for yourself and living in them until they are sold is that, in most localities, contractor's licenses are not required for an owner building for his or her own occupancy.

Your own home should be considered the start of your investment program. It is more than a shelter; it is an excellent investment. Today, buying the best home you can afford in the best area makes sense. This type of home will both provide you with maximum appreciation and increase your general quality of life.

OWNING PROPERTY IN DIFFERENT AREAS

I recently had a student who was a retired Air Force officer. He had purchased a house at each of his U. S. assignments which he has kept. His primary concern for each of his purchases was that it be in a good location. In twenty-five years of service he acquired seven homes, each of which he turned over to local real estate management firms for rental whenever he was transferred. Because of inflation he now has a positive cash flow of over $900 a month and equity in the homes of close to half a million dollars. His total cash downpayments for the seven homes was less than $15,000.

He loves to travel and has friends all over the country, so his investments have a side benefit. On his frequent trips he checks up on his properties, which makes a great deal of his travel expense tax deductible.

While for this retired officer owning rental property at great distances has been successful, I would advise owning rental homes within easy traveling of your residence so that you can handle tenant and property problems more easily. When you invest in a number of single-family dwellings, it saves you a lot of energy if they are located close to each other.

VACATION HOMES

After their first home, the next step for many investors is a vacation home. Today a vacation home can be more of an investment than a luxury. The fact that interest and property taxes are tax deductible helps to offset the cost of keeping a second home. Assume a couple is in the 50 percent tax bracket for the top dollar of their income (both federal and state taxes). If they have a house payment of $650, including taxes and insurance, the chances are that $600 of that payment is deductible interest and taxes. The net effect is that it actually only costs them $350 per month in cash to keep their second home. This would probably be more than offset by appreciation.

If you live in a vacation home for fourteen days a year or less, you can take depreciation on it. If you use it for more than fourteen days, you are not allowed depreciation. Therefore, many owners use their vacation home only a few weekends a year and rent it at other times in order to make depreciation.

The Sunbelt is the best area for vacation homes, as they can there generally be rented more months of the year than in the North and are more readily sold because of the increasing demand for housing in this growing region.

I have two vacation homes. One is a lakeshore home in northern Wisconsin which I use for three months a year. I do not rent it in the off season, but I feel that my appreciation has far exceeded my expenses. In addition it gives me a great deal of pleasure. My other vacation home is a condominium in Lake Havasu, Arizona, which I currently rent. I don't intend to use it until I retire. The rent comes within thirty dollars of making my payments each month, but because of depreciation I am actually over a thousand dollars ahead of the game each year by owning this property. In addition, my appreciation in the last two years has been over 25 percent of the cost and over 100 percent of my investment.

FIXER-UPPERS

Homes in need of a great deal of repair can be excellent investments, especially if you have the time and basic skills to accomplish the necessary work yourself. Generally, the dirtier the property is, the better the deal you can make. Property in rough shape can often be purchased at a good price and on very attractive terms. Often property like this is being foreclosed, is part of an estate or has been foreclosed and is held by the lender.

Before buying these fixer-uppers, check them out carefully to see what must be done. In particular check the plumbing, electrical and heating-cooling systems. Consider carefully what the repairs will cost. Generally, cleaning, painting and yard work can make a big difference in value and saleability. Every dollar spent on a fixer-upper can mean many dollars in profit.

APARTMENT RENTALS

Small rental units such as duplexes and fourplexes offer the advantage of your living in one unit and having the tenants help buy the property through their rents. While rentals will seldom be sufficient to make the payments, the additional cash needed for the payment will often be less than would be required for a comparable single-family home. Excellent financing is usually available for these smaller units.

While you cannot take depreciation on your own apartment, you can depreciate the other units in the building. This will often result in a net positive cash flow when income tax liability is considered. Smaller apartments have an advantage in that, because of demand, they are usually more readily saleable than larger units would be. Nevertheless, larger apartments can be excellent investments.

Problem Properties.   Generally you can expect the highest return from units which give you the greatest problems. Units in run-down areas or units which have collection or tenant difficulties provide higher rates of return than do quality units. However, problem apartments usually have far less appreciation than the better, more trouble-free units, so as a buyer of these types of units you are substituting present income for later appreciation.

One big advantage of troubled units is that owners frequently are very motivated to sell and often will sell with low and even no downpayment. To take advantage of these situations, you must have the time, maintenance skills and interpersonal skills necessary to deal with the tenants.

I know a very young investor who, while a freshman at college, found that the rooming house he lived in was for sale. The owner, a businessman, had purchased it a year earlier. What looked good on paper had turned out to be a nightmare for him. Besides rent collection problems he had constant maintenance, health orders from the city and generally a lot of grief. This student offered the owner $2,000 for his equity, which was accepted. He obtained the $2,000 from his parents by telling them the rooming house would pay for the rest of his education.

The young student evicted several troublemakers and commenced to clean the place up. He now owns eighteen rooming houses in a university city. They are rented to students only. He has a full-time maintenance man and a student manager at each house. His full-time job is watching over his investments. This is not bad for starting with a borrowed $2,000.

Slum Property.   This is of course the most troublesome of all properties. The dangers from vandalism, fear of visiting the property and high insurance rates make ownership unpleasant and often unprofitable. Owners are actually abandoning slum properties because of the many problems involved. Most people do not have the temperament to own such properties.

COMMERCIAL PROPERTY ON LITTLE OR NO DOWNPAYMENT

Investors love good commercial buildings with a long-term lease from a major tenant. However, if you are starting with little or no cash, these investments will usually be beyond your reach. But when commercial property has been vacant for a long period of time, owners are often willing to sell with little or no downpayment. Even when the owner wants a substantial downpayment for a vacant commercial building, it can often be purchased with little cash.

With limited capital to invest, you should consider leasing a property with the right to sublease it. You would want to negotiate a one-year lease with options to renew for a fairly long time, such as two five-year terms. You also want the option to buy the property at an agreed price during at least the first few years of the lease. Your lease should be negotiated at what you consider to be a favorable rental based on other rentals in the area.

You are now obligated to meet lease payments for one year. If you can sublease the property for more than your lease payment, you will have a positive cash flow. At worst, your downside risk is the rental payments for the one year.

If you can find a good tenant and can obtain a long-term sublease (remember you have renewal options), then the value of the building will increase based on the lease. You can now try to sell the building and exercise the option to purchase when you find a buyer.

As an alternative you might be able to exercise the option to purchase without having to sell the property. Based on the lease, if it is to a tenant with financial strength, you could obtain 100 percent financing because the value of the building with the tenant should be far greater than the option price. With a strong tenant, you might be able to obtain financing in excess of the option price. This would mean that you would have not only purchased a property without a downpayment, it would also have given you spendable cash.

I have a friend who worked for me in a rental and property management business. He was an excellent rental agent and was able to rent property other agents considered unrentable. He left my office, lured away by the larger commissions offered in sales. Later, he returned to rentals in an unusual way. He would look for problem properties and agree to rent them on a one-year lease with several renewal options for longer periods. The leases allowed him to sublease. The type of property he looked for usually offered limited-use possibilities and had therefore been vacant for a long period of time. He would offer really minimum rental terms which were often accepted. Now his job was to find a tenant. The method he used was quite simple. He would go through the yellow pages of the local phone book for business categories he thought might be able to use the property. He would call each firm listed in those categories and make his rental pitch. He simply stayed on the phone day after day until he succeeded. In many cases the difference between what he was obligated to pay in rent and what he received was substantial. His downside risk was never more than one year's rent. In just a few years my former employee had become very wealthy. His only complaint was that he had to pay regular income tax, not capital gains, on his profit.

If you don't want to risk signing a lease with options, it is possible to obtain a short-term option to rent coupled with an option to purchase. What you have done is to purchase for a few dollars a period of time to find a tenant.

THE BIGGER THE PROBLEM, THE GREATER THE REWARD

Generally, the bigger the problem of rental, the greater the profit potential in solving the problem. You should analyze a property. Ask who could use it. Then use my friend's method. Go through the yellow pages of a local phone book; it will give you all kinds of ideas as to possible tenants.

I know of a "white elephant" which had been vacant for many years. It had been a central city major department store. An investor finally rented the space on a long-term lease and a very low rental. He took about half the space and rented it to small merchants who really owned their own departments in a department store. Much of the marginal space he partitioned into locked storage areas which he rented as warehouse space. The net effect was a very positive cash flow.

You might think that this investor took a big risk. Actually the risk was comparatively small since he leased the building through a separate corporation. He therefore had no individual liability. If the investor had been unable to sublease the space, he could have walked away with his only loss being the money he had invested in his corporation. I personally do not approve of the ethics of this type of dealing.

While offering greater risk, many investors are buying older commercial property close to the central areas of larger cities. In many cases these properties are in poor condition or have vacancy problems, so they frequently can be purchased for a low or no downpayment. If these properties can be made to break even, they offer profit potential based on changes in the cities. Central urban locations are becoming desirable for large apartment units. Property that a few years ago was barely saleable at any price in some cases is now worth millions. We are seeing in many areas a revitalization of the central city. Because of fuel shortages, long commuting time and a desire by many younger people to live "where it's at," central city property is undergoing a rapid appreciation.

THE VACANCY FACTOR

Office buildings generally require substantial downpayments unless they have high vacancy. Often older buildings lose their tenants to newer ones. Some owners panic when they see their vacancy factor increasing dramatically and may be receptive to offers with very low downpayments.

I know of one investor who constantly checks with General Services Administration for federal agency space needs, as well as with city, county and state real estate departments as to their needs. Governmental agencies usually require large square footage but can seldom pay enough for quality buildings. The investor then locates vacant spaces which he feels from experience and talking to officials will meet the government requirements. His next step is an option to lease the space at as reasonable a rental as he can negotiate. He then tries to rent the space to the government. If he is successful, he can make the difference in his rental and what he can collect from the government. If not, he has lost the amount he paid for the option plus a little time. He has learned government needs to the point where he is right at least 25 percent of the time.

INDUSTRIAL PROPERTY

Industrial property is difficult to deal in because prospective tenants are far fewer than you would find for commercial or residential property. While well-leased industrial property is highly saleable, vacant industrial property requires problem solving. Many industrial buildings were built for particular uses. If you can find the right tenant for the property, you can make a good profit.

LAND

A home in the country with several acres sounds idyllic. It can also be a super investment. Besides the house you have land which will increase in value. Often a home and acreage will cost little if any more than a home in the city. But don't expect to make money farming a few acres. Many people who thought they would live off the land have done so but not in the way they expected to. They found that their land values had so accelerated, they achieved financial independence not by living on the land but by selling it.

Farms and Ranches. These have been excellent investments for many because of depreciation and appreciation. Investors can take depreciation on all of the improvements to the land but not the land itself. In addition, orchards can also be depreciated.

Because of the growth of most of our cities there has been an increased demand for farmland not just for development but also for gentlemen farmers who wish to live a rural life within commuting distance of the city. Good farmland is being lost by development. This loss increases the demand and therefore the price of existing farms. This demand has been fueled by foreign investment in our farmland. In particular, German, French and Italian investors have contributed to our farmland appreciation. As high as we may think our prices are, our farmland is considered a bargain by the rest of the world.

While there are federal loans to buy farmland, generally farm purchases require substantial downpayments. The only exception is marginal farmland, or land which is completely raw and has never been under cultivation. With the high farmland prices, a purchaser who is not going to personally farm the land should not expect the income to make the payments.

Raw Land.   Many investors like raw land since it offers excellent appreciation potential plus the advantage of no management problems. If there are no tenants and no structures, there are few things that can go wrong. Raw land is of course a negative cash flow investment. Your income should be sufficient to make your payments. Since most of the payments are applied to interest which is deductible, the higher your income the less it really costs you to buy raw land. Owners customarily finance the buyers on raw land sales. In many areas 10 percent down is common. Sellers will often carry the balance at interest rates far less than market interest.

Raw land sales have attracted many sharp operators who want to sell you small parcels at prices far greater than the land is worth. There have been many fraud convictions for this type of sale. I have advised owners to stop making payments on land when after several years they still owe far more than the land is worth.

Raw land is the most illiquid of all investments. It is difficult to borrow on and very often difficult to sell. Many parcels take several years to sell. While raw land in many cases has increased in value several thousand percent in short periods of time, it is more speculative than other investments. Therefore, it should be only a part of any investment plan.

Improved Lots.   Because of the costs of large parcels, some investors buy improved lots. While lots generally offer a lower profit potential than raw land, the profit can nevertheless be substantial. In periods of high interest rates and low building activity, bargain prices are possible on residential lots. In addition, the seller usually finances the buyer with a low downpayment. An advantage of improved lots over raw land is that lots are usually more readily saleable than raw land.

One danger to recognize in buying land is that zoning can be changed. A change in zoning can mean a change in value. A change from residential zoning to commercial zoning could result in a substantial increase in value, while a change from commercial to residential zoning would have serious adverse effects on the value of the land.

As you can see, real estate investment covers a wide range of opportunities. You may have discovered that you are already a real estate investor but didn't realize it. Real estate can provide for your future: let it be the foundation. Remember, "under all is the land."

The spirit of property doubles a man's strength.
—Voltaire, 1764

3

Taxation and Real Estate

With our progressive income tax, the more money you make, the more taxes you pay. As your regular income increases, the increases are taxed as increasingly higher tax rates. Because the federal tax brackets have not been indexed for inflation, a cost-of-living increase really means your take-home pay is actually lower in terms of purchasing power. As wages go up, higher percentages are taken for taxes.

It has therefore become extremely difficult to accumulate substantial savings from a salary alone. Even when you are able to save, our tax laws tax the interest you earn as ordinary income, raising you still further up in the federal and state tax brackets. Our tax laws really have the net effect of penalizing people who are able to increase their earnings or who are able by thrift to save and earn interest on their savings.

Tax evasion is a federal crime, but tax avoidance is not only legal, it is just good common sense. It is possible for an investor to work within the tax laws and pay little if any income taxes and yet have significant spendable income.

CAPITAL GAINS

Our capital gains laws allow us the opportunity to exempt 60 percent of the gain on the sale of real estate from federal income taxes. If an asset is held for over one year, it qualifies for this special capital gains treatment.

Assume you purchase a lot for $10,000 and sell it over one year later for $20,000. You would now have a long-term capital gains of $10,000. Sixty percent of the gain is exempt from federal taxation, so you would add only 40 percent of the gain, or $4,000 to your other income. If the income was in the 30 percent tax bracket, you would pay 30 percent of the $4,000 or $1,200 in taxes. If the $10,000 gain had been regular income, your taxes would have been $3,000.

The savings become more significant as your income increases. If you

18

were in the 70 percent tax bracket, the highest federal tax bracket for investment income, you would pay 70 percent of $4,000, or $2,800, in taxes on a $10,000 gain. If that $10,000 gain had been received as regular income, the tax would have been $7,000. The tax benefit of capital gains could even increase as there is legislative pressure to raise the capital gains tax exemption to 70 percent. Since most states have state income taxes and capital gains exclusions, difference between capital gains and regular income can be even greater. With a state tax as well as the maximum 70 percent federal tax, the tax bite for regular income doesn't leave much left for the taxpayer. While 70 percent is the maximum tax rate for investment income, the maximum federal tax rate for wages is 50 percent.

CAPITAL GAINS OR REGULAR INCOME?

Some taxpayers have found that what they thought was a long-term capital gain turned out to be regular income. Property must be held for over one year; a hold for one year or less is not enough. In order to make a gain qualify as long term, it is possible to open a long escrow which does not close until the one-year period has been exceeded.

People who are in the business of buying and selling real estate for profit are not entitled to take capital gains. The IRS considers developers and others who buy and sell as a normal business to be "dealers." Dealers' gains are taxed as regular income. I have heard one accountant say, "You are not a dealer until the IRS says you are one." Some people who could benefit by having real estate licenses do not obtain them because they are afraid it might call the attention of the IRS to their dealing and mean the loss of their capital gains. They don't want to be found to be in the business of buying and selling real estate. While the IRS definition of a dealer is apparently fairly subjective, you are unlikely to be considered a dealer unless you buy and sell significant amounts of real estate or sell a number of pieces with holding periods of only slightly more than one year. This could be a red flag for an IRS auditor. If you buy and sell only a couple of properties each year and maintain other employment, you are unlikely to be classified as a dealer. If you are in doubt as to whether you are a dealer, I would recommend that you check with a tax attorney or an accountant.

If you have held land for a period of time and it has significantly increased in value, developing it yourself could be a problem. Since development would be a dealer activity, you could lose your capital gains on the increase in value of the land. To avoid this possibility, you could sell the land to a separate corporation to develop. You would take capital gains on the land, while the corporation would pay regular income tax on the development gain. To avoid the double taxation of corporations (corporations are taxed on corporate profit and the dividends paid are taxed to stockholders), a small corporation can elect to be taxed as a partnership rather than as a corporation.

WHEN YOU SELL YOUR HOME

When you sell your principal residence, you can defer any capital gains tax on the sale if you buy within eighteen months of the sale (before or after) another residence which costs as much or more than you received from the sale of the previous residence. You can also defer your capital gains tax if you start construction of a new residence within eighteen months of the sale and occupy it within two years. Your taxes can thus be deferred for several sales until a residence is finally sold and not replaced.

COMPUTING CAPITAL GAINS

The capital gains tax is computed according to your cost basis. Cost basis is the cost of the residence plus improvements. Improvements are new things such as a patio, a room addition or air conditioning if the house was not previously air-conditioned. Repairs such as a new roof or a new compressor for an air conditioner are generally not considered improvements and do not affect your cost basis.

The following illustrates how the cost base is computed when a homeowner buys and sells homes:

```
1960   House 1 purchased for  .......................... $12,000
       Patio added  ....................................      900
       Fireplace added ................................    1,100
                                    Cost base of house 1: $14,000
1968   House 1 sold for  ............................... $27,000
1968   House 2 purchased for  .......................... $34,000
       Cost base of house 1  ................ $14,000
       Amount added to sale price of house 1
         to buy house 2 ....................    7,000
                          Cost base of house 2: $21,000
1972   House 2 sold for  ............................... $56,000
1972   House 3 purchased for  .......................... $73,000
       Cost base of house 2  ................ $21,000
       Amount added to sale price of house 2
         to buy house 3 ....................   17,000
                          Cost base of house 3: $38,000
1981   House 3 sold for  ............................... $173,000
       No new residence purchased
```

Capital gains would be computed as the difference between the cost base of house 3 ($38,000) and its selling price ($173,000). The capital gains therefore is $135,000.

$173,000   net sales price
− 38,000   cost base
$135,000   long-term capital gains

Since under capital gains a person has a 60 percent exemption, only 40 percent of the $135,000 would be added to the other income to determine the tax. Forty percent of $135,000 is $54,000, so the taxpayer would show an additional $54,000 in income for the year of the sale.

BENEFITS FOR OLDER TAXPAYERS

For taxpayers fifty-five years of age or older, the IRS allows a lifetime exclusion of $100,000 providing the taxpayer has occupied the residence for three of the preceding five years. This means that $100,000 of the gain is not subject to any federal income tax. In the case above, the $100,000 exclusion would reduce the taxable gain to $35,000 ($135,000 less the $100,000 exclusion). For tax purposes the taxpayer would add 40 percent of the $35,000, or $14,000, to the other income. Some states have similar $100,000 capital gains exemptions for senior taxpayers selling their principal residence.

If you were fifty-three years of age or older and intended to sell the residence you had lived in for at least three years, and if you did not intend to buy a new residence, then you would want to delay completion of the sale until you were fifty-five. You could do this through a long escrow.

The $100,000 exemption is a one-time exemption. If either the husband or wife has ever taken the exemption before, then the new spouse, in case of another marriage, would be precluded from taking it. One accountant I know says he might suggest in such a case that the couple get divorced so that the second spouse can take the exemption.

As you can see, our tax laws really favor home ownership. A home today is much more than shelter. If you own your own home, you are already a real estate investor.

CAPITAL LOSS

If you take a loss on the sale of real property other than your residence, you can take a capital loss. You can use the loss to offset other capital gains. If you have no capital gains, you can use $3,000 of the loss each year, carrying it forward until it is used up. Each two dollars of loss will shelter one dollar of other income from taxation.

Tax laws are not necessarily fair. While a profit on the sale of your residence is considered a capital gain, a loss on the sale of your residence is not recognized. One way to protect yourself is to change the character of your residence. Some accountants suggest you move out of your residence and rent it out for at least one year. Other accountants recommend that it be rented for a longer period, preferably longer than two years. This changes the character of the property from a residence to investment property. A capital loss on the sale of investment property is recognized by the IRS.

INSTALLMENT SALES

Installment sales offer another tax advantage. If you receive sale proceeds over a number of years, you can spread your capital gains out over the period in which your profit is received. Because of our progressive tax, a very large gain in one year will push your income into a higher tax bracket. By spreading the gain over several years, you can keep your income in a lower bracket. This is especially important for people now having large earnings who intend to retire in a few years. They can collect their gain during their retirement years when their other income is reduced, and thereby pay relatively little income tax even on a substantial gain.

Installment sales can benefit you as a buyer also. Once they understand the tax advantages of installment sales, owners who had been asking for cash can be influenced to sell excellent investment property with relatively low downpayments.

Until fairly recently, in order to qualify as an installment sale, the seller had to receive 30 percent or less of the sale price in the year of the sale. In order to play it safe, many owners would require 29 percent downpayments. Even though the tax laws have changed, allowing the property to be taxed in the years received regardless of the amount of downpayment, many owners are unaware of the change and still stick to the old 29 percent downpayment requirement.

INCOME AVERAGING

Another way to avoid the tax burden on an unusually high income in one year is to take advantage of income averaging on your income tax. You should compute your tax liability both ways—with and without income averaging. Whichever method gives you the lowest tax liability can then be used.

Leverage. One of the reasons many investors like unimproved land is leverage. The seller is usually willing to finance the buyer with a very low downpayment. For people with low incomes this type of investment has little appeal, but people in higher tax brackets can receive great tax benefits from such investments.

Assume you are in the 50 percent federal income tax bracket and you wish to invest in twenty acres of land at $10,000 per acre. The total investment would therefore be $200,000. If it could be purchased with 10 percent down, you would be financing $180,000. Assume the seller is agreeing to accept interest-only payments for six years at a 10 percent interest rate. Your yearly payments would be $18,000. If the taxes were $2,000, your yearly outlay to hold the property would be $20,000. Since the entire $20,000 is deductible as taxes and interest expenses and you are in the 50 percent tax bracket, your actual net cost to keep the property is only $10,000 per year. This is without figuring state income tax advantages, which will reduce your net cost even more. Even if your payments were amortized, since most of the money in the early years goes toward interest, the difference between this figure and your real net cost to hold the property would not be significant.

If you were in the 70 percent federal income tax bracket, your real out-of-pocket cost to hold the property in the above case would be only 30 percent, or $6,000 per year. This would be reduced even further since interest payments and taxes are also deductible items for state income taxes. Uncle Sam really picks up most of the tab when payments are primarily toward interest and taxes and you are in a higher tax bracket.

DEPRECIATION FOR TAX PURPOSES

Many investors look for depreciation since depreciation is treated as an expense for tax purposes. While only a paper expense since an owner pays nothing out, the expense offsets or shelters other income from taxation. Unfortunately, some investors buy a tax shelter first rather than analyzing the outlay as an investment. Anyone can get a tax break because they lost money on a venture. It doesn't take much intelligence to lose your entire investment. Don't buy a tax shelter; buy the total investment. Your first consideration should be: Is it a good investment? Look at the investment from the standpoint of appreciation and income. Depreciation is the frosting on the cake.

The IRS realizes assets such as an apartment building will not last forever. They therefore allow an owner to deduct an amount as depreciation which allows the owner to recoup the investment. Each year the investor deducts the amount of depreciation taken from the book value of the property.

Ten years ago there were many available investments which would yield a good cash return. Because of inflation, a great number of people wished to protect their assets by investing in real estate. The principle of supply and demand led to many improved properties being sold at prices and terms which resulted in negative cash flows. These properties were not sold based on their income at the time of sale; their sale prices were based on the anticipated future income which would result from continued inflation and the resulting increase in value. A large negative cash flow at the time of purchase often turned into a substantial positive cash flow and a substantial increase in value in just a few years.

For many buyers the net effect of large negative cash flows can be negligible. First of all, the actual cash loss could be offset in part or in full by depreciation. If there is still a loss after depreciation is considered, the government helps pay for the loss by allowing the loss to shelter other income.

Let us assume a property has an operational loss of expenses over income of $10,000 per year. If the property also allows $5,000 for depreciation, the loss would be $15,000. If the owner is in a 50 percent federal income tax bracket, the actual cash loss is reduced to $2,500 since the loss shelters $15,000 of other income. If the owner were in the 70 percent federal tax bracket, the loss saves $10,500 in tax expenditures, so the net effect of ownership is $500 a year in nontaxed income for the owner.

Depreciation lowers a property's book value, which means a greater profit on the sale for tax purposes. Your capital gains tax is based on the difference between book value and sales price. Depreciation really allows you to convert regular income, which is taxed at a normal rate, to capital gains, which is taxed at a reduced rate, and to defer this tax until the property is sold.

To illustrate, assume you purchased a property for $100,000, which you have depreciated to $50,000. By depreciating the building, you sheltered $50,000 from regular income tax. If you now sell the property for $100,000, it would not be a break-even sale since book value has been reduced. You would show a $50,000 long-term capital gains of which 60 percent would be exempt from taxation. You can see why it is still profitable to buy and sell property even when you only sell it for what you paid for it. Instead of paying full income tax on your earnings, you are able to use the money and defer the tax liability. When you finally sell, you only have to pay 40 percent of the taxes you would have had to pay for regular income. Of course most property has in the past appreciated a great deal in value and should continue to do so.

DEPRECIATION METHODS

Depreciation for real estate investments may be computed by either the (1) straight line method, (2) declining balance method, or (3) sum-of-the-years method. A buyer of property is not concerned with the method used by the previous owner. A buyer picks an appropriate allowable method based on his or her individual needs, and depreciation based on his or her cost.

Straight Line Method. Under this method, which can be used on any property, we depreciate the cost of an improvement over the life of an improvement in equal annual amounts. We never depreciate the land; only manmade improvements such as buildings, fences and orchards can be depreciated. As an illustration, suppose a property is purchased for $125,000 and the land value is $25,000. The amount that could be depreciated would be $100,000. If the property had an expected remaining life of twenty-five years, you would depreciate the property 4 percent per year, $(25\sqrt{100\%} = 4\%)$. You would therefore show $4,000 (4 percent of $100,000) each year as depreciation. In the twenty-fifth year you would depreciate the improvements to zero, so that the book value of the property would be $25,000, the land cost.

Declining Balance Method. This is an accelerated method of depreciation where the rates used are a percentage of the applicable straight line rate. The rates are as follows:

> 200%—to be used only for first user residential income property (property never before been depreciated).
> 150%—to be used for first user property other than residential.
> 125%—to be used for used residential property (property previously depreciated by another owner).
> For all other property the straight line method must be used.

An accelerated method, such as the declining balance method, allows greater depreciation in the early years and less later on. It provides a means to recapture the investment in a shorter period of time.

To illustrate how the declining balance method works, we will apply the 200 percent method (double declining balance) to the situation used under straight line depreciation whereby we depreciated $100,000 over twenty-five years at 4 percent a year. With the 200 percent declining balance method we would use an 8 percent figure (200 percent of the straight line rate).

In the first year, therefore, we depreciate 8 percent of $100,000.

$$\begin{array}{r} \$100,000 \\ \times\ .08 \\ \hline \$8,000 \end{array}$$

First year depreciation:

For the second year we depreciate 8 percent of the declining balance of $92,000 ($100,000 less $8,000):

$$\begin{array}{r} \$\ 92,000 \\ \times\ .08 \\ \hline \$7,360 \end{array}$$

Second year depreciation:

For the third year we depreciate from a balance of $84,640 ($92,000 less $7,360):

$$\begin{array}{r} \$\ 84,640 \\ \times\ .08 \\ \hline \end{array}$$

Third year depreciation: $6,771.20

As you can see, under this method depreciation is more rapid during the early years. As the years go by you will get less and less depreciation. You generally should switch from the declining balance method to the straight line method when the declining balance depreciation has declined to the amount of the straight line depreciation. You can change from an accelerated depreciation method to the straight line method, but you require IRS approval to change from straight line to accelerated depreciation.

Even though a property has never been depreciated for tax purposes, an owner could be precluded from taking first owner depreciation if a previous owner, such as a builder, was eligible to take depreciation. The IRS would regard it as if it had been taken, thus precluding a subsequent owner from taking the first owner depreciation. In the same vein, if the previous owner were not eligible to take depreciation, a later owner could take it.

As an example, if you purchased a house that had previous owners but had never been used for rental purposes, it would never have been depreciated. You might therefore be eligible for 200 percent declining balance depreciation even though the house was not new.

Component Depreciation. Even greater depreciation can be taken by using component depreciation. Component depreciation can be used with straight line depreciation as well as with declining balance depreciation. Using this method, you depreciate elements of the building according to their various effective lives. A building having a cost base of $100,000 might be depreciated as follows:

	Value	*Life*
Structure	$62,000	30 years
Electrical	8,000	12 years
Plumbing	14,000	15 years
Air conditioning	7,000	8 years
Roof	9,000	10 years

In using this method, you simply determine the depreciation separately for each component and then add them up.

By depreciating some components over shorter periods, you can gain a great deal more depreciation during the early years. I recommend that you obtain a professional appraisal from a qualified appraiser and base your values on the appraisal. Some accountants do not recommend component depreciation since they feel it is a flag for an IRS audit. I recommend, however, that you consider following the lead of the many successful investors who use this method.

Sum-of-the-Years or Sum-of-the-Digits Method. This method can be used only for new residential property which has never before been depreciated. To use this accelerated method, we first add up the years. Assume a sauna has a life of ten years. We would add up:

$$1 + 2 + 3 + 4 + 5 + 6 + 7 + 8 + 9 + 10 = 55$$

To depreciate the asset, we now form a fraction and go backwards as follows:

1st year— $\frac{10}{55}$
2nd year— $\frac{9}{55}$
3rd year— $\frac{8}{55}$
4th year— $\frac{7}{55}$
5th year— $\frac{6}{55}$
6th year— $\frac{5}{55}$
7th year— $\frac{4}{55}$
8th year— $\frac{3}{55}$
9th year— $\frac{2}{55}$
10th year— $\frac{1}{55}$

We are therefore able to depreciate $\frac{55}{55}$ or 100 percent of the cost of the asset over the ten years with the greatest depreciation during the early years. Since this method and the 200 percent and 150 percent declining balance methods are available only for first owners, you can readily understand the advantage of first owner depreciation.

WHICH DEPRECIATION METHOD SHOULD YOU USE?

If you only expect to hold a property a few years, you should discuss the appropriate depreciation method with a CPA. The reason for this is that if you sell and the depreciation you have taken exceeds what would have been taken by the straight line method, then the excess depreciation could be taxed as regular income.

Most new structures have a life of from forty to fifty years. Forty years is generally acceptable by the IRS. In some instances you might want to take a far shorter life, such as for a very cheaply constructed building or a temporary structure. A building to be erected on leased land could be depreciated over the term of the lease even though the building would have a much greater life. If you are using an unusually short life for depreciation, your tax return should fully explain why the shorter life was used. An unusually short depreciation life will be a red flag to an IRS auditor.

For second-owner buildings some accountants recommend twenty-five years, while others say you can go as low as twenty years. Generally, any depreciation life less than twenty years would be questioned by the IRS.

Since you will want to take the greatest depreciation possible, the ratio of land value to improvement value is of great importance. Some people get comparable land sales or have an appraiser appraise the value of the land. (Remember, land cannot be depreciated; you can only depreciate the improvements.)

Often an easier and better way in terms of results is to use the last property tax bill. The tax bill will show the assessed tax value of the land and improvements separately. Usually the land is given a comparatively low value. As an example, a property you buy for $100,000 might actually have a $25,000 land value based on comparable sales. The property might be assessed at only $40,000 for the improvements and $3,000 for the land. The land value is then only 6.96 percent of the total assessed value of $43,000. You could therefore take this percentage of the purchase price, or $6,967, as the land value and use $93,033 as the value of the improvements.

The IRS will normally go along with this apportionment of value. Even though they may not be realistic, the IRS will generally respect decisions made by another governmental body as to value apportionment. In a few instances, assessors have placed too great a value on the land and not enough on the improvements. In cases such as this, I recommend you obtain a fee appraisal and use the appraiser's ratio of land to improvement value.

I have a very simple system for keeping records. I set up a separate bank checking account for each of my properties. I deposit all of my income from a property into the account and pay bills from the account. If the account gets too large, I transfer some money to a savings account. If I need more money, I transfer more in. I also keep a nine-by-twelve-inch envelope for all bills connected with each property. These records are sufficient to complete operational statements at the end of each year for my benefit and to prepare and justify tax returns.

As you progress in your real estate investments, you will see that taxes play an ever greater role in your decision making. The tax laws are a two-edged sword; they can benefit you. Be honest in your dealings with the IRS but don't give them one cent more than you have to. If you want to give money away, give it to charity. Charitable gifts are deductible, but you get no deductions for gifts to the IRS.

The best investment on earth is earth.

—*Louis Glickman, 1957*

4

Understanding Financing

It is unusual for a buyer of real estate to pay cash for a purchase. Besides the fact that the amount of cash required is very large, a cash purchase normally is not good business. The average sale is financed either by an individual, in the case of the seller financing the buyer, or by a lending institution. Lending institutions use money supplied by savers who are satisfied with a comparatively low rate of return coupled with safety. By using financing to buy real estate, you use other people's money (OPM) to make money for yourself.

METHODS OF FINANCING

The three primary instruments of financing are mortgages, trust deeds and land contracts.

Mortgages. A mortgage is a two-party instrument in which the mortgagor (borrower) gives a promissory note and a mortgage to a mortgagee (lender).

Mortgagor	Mortgage ⟶	Mortgagee
(borrower)	Note ⟶	(lender)

In most states the mortgage is regarded as a lien. In a few states the mortgage is regarded as an actual transfer of title to secure the loan.

While the mortgagee is customarily a lending institution such as a savings and loan association, when the seller finances the buyer, the seller is the mortgagee and takes a mortgage as security for the balance of the purchase price.

A mortgage is recorded with the county recorder. Once recorded, it gives notice of the mortgagee's interest in the mortgaged property. When the

29

mortgagor pays off the mortgage, the mortgagee gives the mortgagor a satisfaction of the mortgage, which is also recorded. Once the satisfaction of mortgage is on record, the mortgagee's interest in the mortgaged property is terminated.

Should the mortgagor default on the payments or fail to pay the taxes or insurance, the mortgagee can foreclose on the mortgage. Generally, the mortgagor is given a period of redemption in which to pay off the loan and thereby keep the property. The usual period for mortgage redemption is one year.

When a mortgage is foreclosed, the property is sold at auction. If the sale brings less than the amount owing to the mortgagee, in some states it is possible to get a deficiency judgment against the mortgagor for the balance. However, in many states deficiency judgments are either not possible or are very difficult to obtain. I recommend that you check with an attorney in your state to determine your state's laws and the attitude of the courts toward deficiency judgments.

Trust Deeds.   In order to avoid the lengthy redemption period allowed for a mortgagor in default, a few states have gone to trust deeds. A trust deed is a three-party instrument by which a borrower (trustor) makes payments on a note to a lender (beneficiary). In order to provide the beneficiary with greater security, the trustor actually gives title (a trust deed) to a third person (trustee) to hold.

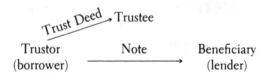

Like the mortgage, the trust deed is recorded to show the interest of the beneficiary. When the trustor has paid the beneficiary in full, the beneficiary orders the trustee to return the title to the trustor. This is done with a deed of reconveyance from the trustee to the trustor. Once the deed of reconveyance is recorded, the interest of the beneficiary is terminated. In the event the trustor defaults, foreclosure is relatively quick. After a short notice period, usually several months, the trustee has a sale and the trustor's interest is lost. After the sale, no redemption period is allowed.

Land Contracts.   A land contract or contract of sale is a two-party instrument in which the vendor (seller) retains title and the vendee (buyer) is merely given possession. The vendee does not receive a deed until the vendor has been paid.

Vendor   Land Contract   Vendee
(seller—   ⟶   (buyer—
retains title)   gets possession)

Land contracts are normally used in situations in which the seller is financing a buyer who is buying with a relatively low downpayment. Since under a land contract the seller retains the best possible security, the title, foreclosure is generally relatively fast and simple. However, foreclosure under a land contract in some states is as time-consuming as for a mortgage.

While most states have legislation to protect the vendee, land contracts can still be dangerous. The vendor might be unable to deliver clear title after the vendee has paid for the property. It is now possible for the vendee under a land contract to obtain title insurance for protection. I recommend such insurance very strongly. The vendee should also insist that the land contract be recorded.

The priority of mortgages, trust deeds and land contracts is determined by the time and date of recording. A mortgage which is recorded later than another one on the same property is a second mortgage. The problem with a secondary lien such as a second mortgage is that, should a prior lien be foreclosed, the junior lien is wiped out. In order to protect their interests, holders of junior liens can step in and make the payments on the foreclosing lien, thus stopping foreclosure. They can then foreclose on their junior liens. In this way they end up owning the property with a prior lien on it. If a junior lienholder waits for the foreclosure sale of a prior lien, he or she then has to bid cash to protect his or her interests.

ASSUMING LOANS

When you purchase a property that has an existing loan against it, you can either refinance it, which means that the old loan is paid off and a new loan placed against the property, or you can assume or take subject to the existing loan. When you assume a loan, you agree to be liable for it. Depending on the state, you may be liable for a deficiency judgment should you assume a loan which is later foreclosed and the foreclosure sale yields less than is still owing on the loan. When you take subject to a loan, you recognize that there is a loan against the property and that if you wish to keep the property you will have to make the payments on the loan. However, if you don't make the payments and the property is foreclosed, no deficiency judgment is possible against you because you never agreed to be obligated for the existing loan.

DUE-ON-SALE CLAUSES

Frequently mortgages and trust deeds contain due-on-sale clauses, also known as alienation clauses. They require that the entire balance be paid if the property is sold. A loan with a clause such as this generally cannot be assumed. In California the courts will not allow a lender of a state-licensed institution to declare a loan due unless the lender can show that the loan assumption has impaired his or her security. Several other states appear to be following California's lead in this area.

Courts in several states have held that since a sale by land contract does not involve a transfer of title, a lender cannot declare a loan due when the mortgagor sells by land contract. However, some states have taken the position that if the due-on-sale clause says "transfer of any interest," then the loan is due even though the sale was by land contract. There are a number of cases pending which are expected to set precedents in this area.

One possible way to get around a due-on-sale clause is a lease option. The tenant (lessee) signs a long-term lease with an agreed-upon portion of the rent applying to the purchase option. In lieu of a downpayment the tenant pays the last few months of the rent in advance. The purchaser can be protected by recording the lease option. To the best of my knowledge, these lease options have not yet been challenged by lenders in court. However, I recommend that you obtain legal advice about using lease options to avoid due-on-sale clauses.

BARGAINING WITH THE LENDER

Even when a loan by its terms cannot be assumed, it is nevertheless possible to bargain with the lender. By threatening to sell on a land contract if an assumption is not allowed, a buyer can often convince the lender to compromise. Lenders might also be willing to rewrite the loan for the new buyer if they can get an increased interest rate. For example, if the going rate is 13 percent, a lender might rewrite an existing 8½ percent loan at an 11½ percent rate. The lender realizes that even though the new rate is lower than the market rate, it is better than having the property resold on a land contract and being stuck with the old rate.

I know of a case in which there was an old 6 percent loan against a property. The loan was assumable. A buyer approached the lender and agreed to pay the current 12 percent rate if the lender would increase the amount of the loan by 70 percent. The lender agreed and in effect gave the purchaser a 100 percent loan on the property.

Lenders with long-term loans at fixed rates of interest will often make concessions to get out of the loans.

PREPAYMENT PENALTIES ON LOANS

Loans frequently have prepayment penalties. The lenders feel that the agreement was for a long-term loan; by wanting to pay the loan off early, the borrower is breaching the agreement. The lenders feel the penalty is justified since it takes time and money to put the money out again earning interest on a real estate loan. Lenders frequently require six months' interest on the loan balance for prepayment.

Lenders will ask for this prepayment penalty even when you wish to prepay a loan which is at a rate of interest below the current market rate. You can often talk a lender into waiving the prepayment penalty by indicating that you don't have to prepay but will only do so if the penalty is waived. If the lender believes that you are selling the property and it will be refinanced, then the lender might very well refuse to waive it. You should then indicate that you will sell by land contract or lease option. These negotiations can become like a poker game: the lender, afraid to call your bluff, may waive the penalty.

If a loan allows payments of a set dollar amount "or more" per month, there can be no prepayment penalty. The borrower has the right to prepay.

While normally only found in personal property loans, some states allow real estate loans to have lock-in clauses. These clauses are vicious because while they allow the borrower to prepay a loan, the borrower must pay all the interest as if the loan had gone to maturity. The borrower is locked into the interest. With a lock-in clause, lenders are frequently willing to negotiate a prepayment penalty much lower than they are entitled to.

TYPES OF LOANS

A hard money loan is a loan in which the lender actually supplies cash. The lender either puts up money for the borrower to buy property or gives an owner money based on the security of the property. Hard money loans bear a high market rate of interest.

A purchase money loan is a loan in which the seller finances the buyer. The seller really carries the loan, or paper. Suppose an owner sells a property to a buyer, taking a downpayment. If the balance of the purchase price were a mortgage given by the purchaser to the seller, then the seller is financing the purchaser.

Sellers will frequently carry the paper on loans at a lower interest rate than would be required for a hard money loan. One reason is that individual sellers cannot usually get a high rate of interest on a long-term investment. If a seller is only getting 9½ percent at a savings and loan association, he or she might be willing to carry paper at 11 percent even though the going mortgage rate is 13 percent. Another reason is that the part of the purchase price carried by the seller is usually mostly profit. Sellers are often so interested in the dollars they will receive as profit that they fail to realize that the interest can be a material part of their profit.

As a seller you can make money on interest differential. For example, suppose you wish to sell your $120,000 property on which you have an old $50,000 mortgage at 6 percent interest. You sell the property with $20,000 down on a land contract at 12 percent interest. You would now be getting 12 percent interest on your $50,000 equity plus a 6 percent interest differential over the $50,000 mortgage. This really works out to an 18 percent interest on your equity.

The same net effect can be realized by using a wrap-around loan, also known as an all-inclusive loan. For this type, you would write a new mortgage for the amount of your equity plus the existing loan(s). In the above case, the new mortgage would be for $100,000, and as the seller you would make the payments on the preexisting $50,000 loan.

ARBITRAGE

Arbitrage is the term given to making money on the interest differential when you buy at one interest rate and sell at a higher rate.

About twenty years ago I knew of a couple actively engaged in arbitrage. There were many people who had great difficulty in obtaining home loans at the time. Lenders only considered part of the wages of married women when they were of childbearing age. Single men and single women also had a difficult time obtaining financing, as did minorities.

This couple had excellent credit and purchased a great number of homes, obtaining excellent financing. The couple resold the homes with the identical downpayments they had paid, but asking a 10 percent increase in price plus a 2 percent interest differential. They found many trustworthy buyers who had been unable to obtain financing on their own and were eager for this chance to own homes.

On each $10,000 of their purchase price, the couple would obtain $1,000 in profit plus the interest on it. If they were obtaining 9 percent interest on a twenty-year loan, the total payments for the $1,000 profit would amount to $2,160. The 2 percent interest differential on each $10,000 of the land contract over a twenty-year loan period amounts to $3,086. Therefore, for each $10,000 in loans the couple agreed to be obligated on, they would receive a total of $5,246 in interest and profit over the period of the loan. The best part was that they had none of their own money left in the transaction. Using this simple formula, the couple purchased and resold over fifty homes. They had only one foreclosure, which they actually resold at a profit. The interest differential on well over one million dollars in loans became their own retirement annuity.

For you as a seller, it can be far more advantageous to sell on land contract or with a wrap-around loan than to have the buyer assume a low-interest loan and give you a second mortgage for the balance. Of course, if you are a buyer, you would want to assume the existing loan and give the seller a second mortgage for the balance of the purchase price.

DISCOUNTING

As interest rates rise, private holders of mortgages become unhappy with their long-term investments at low rates of return. Frequently they were not too happy to carry the paper in the first place and only did so because it appeared necessary to consummate a sale. While the private mortgage holder may have a great deal of money due, it doesn't seem like much the way it comes in monthly dribbles. Often a person holding paper would like to see a sizable amount of cash for once. Such mortgagees are prime candidates for discounting. They can often be induced to sell their paper for less than the face value. Because the paper normally represents a profit, discounting isn't viewed as taking a loss; it is just a reduction in profit.

Several years ago I received a cash offer on a property I owned which had three loans against it. I went to my mortgagees and made offers to pay them off for a cash discount. Two agreed and the net effect was more than $5,000 in discounts. The discounts I received made the purchase offer more attractive, and I made the sale.

A few years ago in the period of one month I was paid in full on two low-interest, second mortgages I was holding because the properties were being sold and the buyers were obtaining their own financing. If I had been asked, I would have jumped at accepting a 25 percent discount. As it was, I was paid in full.

If there are several assumable loans, it can be smart to assume them even if you intend to refinance the property. After you buy the property and have assumed the loans, you should try for a discount. If the holders agree to it, then you refinance.

PRIMARY FINANCING

Primary financing refers to first mortgages and trust deeds. These loans are usually made by institutional lenders such as banks, savings and loan institutions and insurance companies. Banks generally prefer short-term, high-interest loans. They therefore like construction loans which seldom exceed two years and bear a high interest rate. They will also finance personal property such as furniture involved in a sale. Savings and loan associations make the majority of home loans because they are allowed to give a high loan-to-value ratio.

Insurance companies like large loans preferably on new property. These companies realize that they can often get much more than interest for the use of their money. For many loans they demand equity participation. They actually become a partner with the borrower and share in the profits while still receiving interest on the loan.

SAM.   Several home lenders are experimenting with a similar loan for homes. They are offering loans at several percentage points below the market rate of interest but asking for a 30 to 50 percent equity share in any profit when the house is sold. These loans generally require the mortgagor to refinance or sell within a stated period of time. These loans are generally known as SAM (Sharing Appreciation Mortgages).

Such loans can be beneficial for would-be homeowners who otherwise would be precluded from owning homes by high interest rates. But for an investor, if we assume even a modest rate of appreciation, these loans become far too expensive. You are much better off paying a few percentage points more in interest, which is a deductible expense, and keeping all the profit. As a partner, the lender under a SAM does not carry his own weight. This kind of partner you don't need.

SECONDARY FINANCING

Secondary financing refers to second mortgages and trust deeds. In the case of purchase money loans, the loans are carried by the seller. Otherwise they are made by noninstitutional lenders. Noninstitutional lenders include private individuals, mortgage brokers, union pension funds and trusts. Because secondary financing involves a greater risk than first mortgages, the interest rate for these loans is normally higher. As a general rule, the greater the risk, the higher the interest rate the lender will demand. In many states usury laws limit the interest an unlicensed lender can charge to a rate lower than lenders are willing to accept. In these states the sources for hard money through secondary financing have for the most part dried up.

Brokers.   Mortgage loan brokers are active in the secondary financing market. They advertise to the public that it's easy to borrow on a home. They also advertise for investors by emphasizing a high rate of return. The mortgage loan brokers charge commissions and fees for putting borrowers and lenders together.

Besides mortgage brokers, there are charlatans who promise fantastic loans for an advanced fee. Don't be taken in. All the advanced-fee money finders I have heard about found money, but it consisted solely of the fees they collected. For some reason or other, the promised loans never seem to come through.

Balloon Payments. Secondary financing is usually for a short term, such as five to seven years. Often with these loans the regular payments don't pay off the loan; instead there is a huge last payment called a balloon payment. While some people have been foreclosed when they were unable to come up with the final balloon payment, payment is not usually a major problem. With five to seven years of appreciation, the owner's equity has normally increased to the point where new financing is available.

GOVERNMENT LOANS

Government loans are not loans made by the government. They are loans that are either government-insured by the Federal Housing Administration (FHA) or guaranteed by the Veterans Administration (VA). FHA loans are only for housing, including homes, apartments, mobile homes and even mobile parks. VA loans are for homes, farms or businesses. The federal Farmers Home Administration also offers loans. Since government loans are generally made at rates of interest lower than that charged by institutional lenders, they should be considered.

There are a myriad of different types of federal loans available. Some programs are limited by insufficient funds, but many available loans are without takers. The following is only a partial listing of the special loans available: home improvement, single-family homes, farm labor housing, rental housing, housing for the elderly, housing for servicemen, low-income housing, mobile homes, mobile home parks, housing sites, nursing homes, hospitals, medical office buildings, farms, industrial development and recreational enterprises. I strongly recommend that you become familiar with available FHA and Farmers Home Administration programs. For information on FHA loans, write:

> U. S. Department of Housing and
> Urban Development
> Washington, DC 20250

For information on Farmers Home Administration loans, write:
> U. S. Department of Agriculture
> Farmers Home Administration
> Washington, DC 20250

NEW TYPES OF LOANS

In the period before the great depression, most mortgages were straight loans. This means that only interest was paid and when the loans were due, usually in five years, they were customarily rewritten. During the depression, lenders were unable to rewrite these loans, so many people were foreclosed even though they had faithfully made their payments. Because of the problems involved with these straight loans, lenders switched to long-term, amortized loans. These loans were self-liquidating, which means that the equal payments eventually paid off the loan completely.

The federal government has caused rapid changes in our interest rates. The Federal Reserve, which controls the money supply, has raised interest rates as a means of curbing inflation. The theory is that higher interest rates will discourage spending, so that with fewer dollars chasing products, the reduction in demand will keep prices down. The government has taken the opposite approach to curb unemployment. Lower interest rates mean more expansion and employment. Of course, loose credit fuels inflation, which the government then tries to curb by tightening up the money supply again. The government's actions have made interest rates bounce up and down like a yo-yo.

Because of these significant interest fluctuations, lenders are no longer interested in tying up their money in long-term loans at fixed interest rates. Many lenders have found themselves with a majority of outstanding loans at lower interest rates than they now had to pay depositors. This situation made it impossible for the lender to operate at a profit. There are now several new loans designed to protect the lender in periods of great interest fluctuation.

Variable Rate Mortgage (VRM).   This allows the interest rate to be raised or lowered according to the prime rate or some other factor. Usually the number of times a year the rate can be changed and the amount it can be changed are regulated, as are the upper and lower interest limits.

Rollover or Canadian Rollover.   This is a short-term loan usually for five years or less. The payments, however, are based on a long-term amortization such as thirty years. When the loan becomes due, the borrower has the option of paying it off without penalty or agreeing to a new loan at the then current interest rate.

Both of these loans allow lenders to be protected against rising interest rates. I believe that new long-term, fixed interest rate loans will soon be just a memory. The existing long-term fixed interest rate loans which can be assumed will become of great interest to investors. Properties with low-interest, fixed interest rate loans such as these are now selling at premium prices.

Points.   Lenders often require points to make a loan. Each point is equal to 1 percent of the loan. If a lender is requiring ten points to make a $100,000 loan at 13 percent interest, then the lender wants the borrower to come up with

$10,000 for the privilege of getting the loan. For FHA and VA loans, the points are paid by the seller.

Points are charged by lenders when they feel the rate of interest is insufficient. As an example, suppose a lender could make a good, safe, long-term investment at 14½ percent interest and you want a loan at 14 percent. The lender would be foolish to give you a loan at a lower rate of interest than was available elsewhere. By obtaining points, the lender makes up for this differential. As a rule of thumb, eight points are considered equal to a 1 percent interest differential. To give you the loan at a ½ percent interest advantage, the lender will ask for four points. This will give the lender the equivalent of a 14½ percent return.

SHOPPING FOR MONEY

As in buying anything else, you should shop for money. Differences in interest rates, points and loan terms can be significant. Look for the loan that best meets your needs. For example, if you believe interest rates will soon fall and you intend to refinance when that happens, you might not mind paying a premium interest rate on a loan with low points and no prepayment penalty. It would really be just a swing loan to tide you over until you were able to obtain permanent financing at lower interest.

REFINANCING

While real estate is an illiquid investment, it is possible to pump money out of an investment by refinancing a property. As a property increases in value with appreciation, further refinancing is possible.

One Los Angeles investor I know has refinanced the same property four times in a little over ten years. Each time he refinances, he takes more cash out. He uses the cash to pyramid by acquiring more properties. He then refinances the new properties as soon as he is able to take out significant cash. He started on his career by refinancing his home to obtain the downpayment on a fourplex and has continued ever since. While many investors are very conscious of interest rates, this very successful investor is not concerned when he refinances a low-interest loan with a new loan at a much higher rate. He feels that as long as the money costs less than the anticipated return on the new investment, he will be ahead of the game. It is not necessary that the return be in cash. Appreciation in value is also a return on the investment.

This process of borrowing on one property to invest in another offering a rate of return greater than must be paid to borrow the money is known as *trading on your equity.* It is an important tool for pyramiding yourself into more and more properties.

The investor I have told you about never sells, just refinances to increase his holdings. He is not really concerned that refinancing often turns a positive cash flow into a break-even situation, or even into a negative cash flow, as long as he can still make the payments.

It doesn't take experience to borrow money, just a reasonable credit history and property as security. While you may have heard the saying, "Neither a borrower nor a lender be," that advice will get you nowhere. If you want to get ahead today, you must go into debt, but debt well secured by real estate.

When men have yielded without serious resistance to the tyranny of . . . dictators, it is because they have lacked property.
—Walter Lippman
The Method of Freedom

5

Creative Financing

Creative financing is simply financing other than conventional financing. In conventional financing a lender lends money on real estate in return for a promise to repay the loan as well as interest at an agreed rate. In order to secure the loan, the lender usually wants the borrower to have a substantial equity in the property or to be making a substantial downpayment.

Conventional lenders are very concerned with the credit history of the borrower and his or her ability to repay the loan. While a lender wants a loan well secured, the average conventional lender does not want to have to foreclose in order to protect his or her interests. Conventional lenders are primarily interested in money, not in owning real estate.

SELLERS FINANCING BUYERS

Most creative financing involves the seller financing the buyer. The buyer is often able to assume existing loans and give the sellers a second mortgage for their equity. If a seller has no real need for cash, a seller might be persuaded to sell without any downpayment at all if he or she has faith in the buyer. Just because a seller asks for cash doesn't mean that the seller won't sell and carry the paper. If a seller intends simply to invest the sale proceeds in a savings account or bonds, he or she can frequently be induced to carry the paper by the offer of higher interest. After all, the seller knows the security value of the property.

Even if you have the cash to meet the seller's downpayment requirement or to pay off the seller's equity in full, you should conserve your cash. Liquidity offers you protection in an emergency as well as allowing you to take advantage of additional investment opportunities that come along.

While few long-term, fixed-rate loans are being given anymore, there are still many of these loans out at relatively low interest rates. As a buyer, you will want to assume or take subject to these favorable loans. An astute seller will want to sell on a land contract or with a wrap-around loan in order to take advantage of the lower interest rate. Keep in mind that while conventional lenders can be unyielding as to interest rates and terms, rates and terms are usually negotiable when the seller is carrying the loan.

In order to induce a seller to carry a loan, you will probably have to agree to refinance the loan and to pay the seller off within five to seven years. It is difficult to get an average seller to carry the paper for any longer than this.

If an owner indicates that he or she must have a stated amount of money, one solution is to have the owner borrow that amount on the security of the property. You can then assume the new loan or purchase the property on a land contract or a wrap-around loan. If a property is listed through a real estate broker and the owner is asking a low downpayment, such as 10 percent, it is obvious that the seller is really selling for very little or nothing down and is only asking for enough cash to pay the real estate commission. Very low downpayments are common in land sales. If you are interested in a property being sold through a broker with a low downpayment, find out if the broker will accept a commission in the form of a personal note or second mortgage. While some will not agree, many sophisticated brokers will go along with such an arrangement. Your offer to purchase might then state that you are offering a particular price and that you will pay the commission. The seller and the broker together can end up financing you for the entire purchase price.

SUBORDINATION

When you look through ads for lots, you will often see the words "owner will subordinate." In a subordination, the seller not only finances the buyer, but agrees that his or her lien will be secondary or subordinate to another loan. To illustrate, assume that an owner agrees to sell you a lot for $50,000 with $10,000 down and to subordinate a mortgage for $40,000. You could now go to a conventional lender and ask to borrow to build a $100,000 structure. As far as the lender is concerned, you would be asking for a two-thirds loan because the lot, to the lender's way of thinking, is free and clear. The lender, by giving a $100,000 loan, would have the land and building as security under a first mortgage. You have really used the lot seller's equity to finance your loan, even though you have not paid for the lot.

Why would a seller agree to such a deal? If the lender foreclosed, the lot seller would either lose his or her equity or be forced to step in and make the borrower's payments and foreclose on his or her second liens. Some sellers are very motivated. If they are having difficulty making tax payments, they may be willing to subordinate. When there are few sales being made, a seller who has faith in a buyer might agree to subordinate. A buyer with a good reputation in the community or a buyer who has previously purchased property from sellers who subordinated their loans without problems could influence a seller to subordinate.

Often sellers who subordinate are owners of a large number of lots. They want to see some of the lots developed, so as to increase the desirability and value of their other lots. In order to obtain development, they take a calculated risk by subordinating. As an example, several high-priced homes built in a new subdivision will increase the value and desirability of the other lots. Many speculative builders look for subordination opportunities to keep from having their capital tied up in land. Also, by agreeing to subordinate, a seller will often be able to obtain a premium price.

If a seller agrees to subordinate for a particular loan, such as a short-term construction loan, when the construction loan is repaid the seller's loan becomes a primary loan. It would be foolish for a seller to agree to just subordinate without reference to a particular loan, since in such a case the subordinated loan would always be the last in terms of priority.

OTHER WAYS OF BUYING PROPERTY

Some sellers want a substantial downpayment more as a matter of security than because they need the money. In such cases it is possible to supply additional security by manufacturing paper. If you own your home or any other real estate, you can offer a second mortgage on the other property as a downpayment. You created the second mortgage yourself by simply signing it. Chances are, because of inflation, you have a sizable equity in your property. While it might be difficult or very expensive to borrow on your equity, you can use this equity as downpayment material for acquiring more property. The seller not only has the security of the property you have purchased, but also the additional security of the property mortgaged for the downpayment.

If you don't have other property, you may still be able to use property of others to buy property for yourself. If you have relatives or close friends who would help you if they had the cash, you might be able to borrow their paper. I know of a father who put a lien on his home which his son used as a downpayment on a house. The son pays the lien on his father's home as well as the lien on his own. You should realize that you are asking a great deal when you ask to use someone else's property as security for your buying property. There has to be a great deal of trust or love before a person is willing to do this.

One investor has pyramided herself to great wealth. She used her paper equity in property by giving second mortgages as downpayments. As values increase, she gives second mortgages on her most recent acquisitions as well as additional mortgages on other property. She told me she has had as many as five outstanding mortgages on one property. To understand this concept, suppose you owe $40,000 on a house worth $60,000. You give a $10,000 second mortgage on that property as a downpayment on another property. If the value of the original property rises to $80,000, you could then take another mortgage to use as a downpayment on a third property since you have a $30,000 equity. You would now owe $50,000 on a property worth $80,000.

While it is possible to borrow on your property to get cash, you are better off giving the loan directly as a downpayment. Not only can you significantly reduce the interest rates, but you can save the substantial loan costs and commissions necessary to arrange a cash loan.

Some owners will accept "sweat equity" downpayments. Often purchasers of new homes are credited by the builder for tasks such as painting. It reduces the cash downpayment required.

A former student of mine buys "fixer-uppers." He purchased a house with no downpayment from a seller who did not need the cash. The seller nevertheless wanted additional security. The seller agreed to the no-downpayment sale providing the buyer painted the exterior of the house and put in a sprinkler system and lawn. The escrow did not close until the work was completed. With the labor and money the buyer invested in repairs, the seller felt secure with no downpayment. The chances of the seller defaulting were greatly reduced. In addition, the improvements and repairs increased the value of the security.

Some years back it was common to be able to get 100 percent loans if you were building a structure. In fact, many builders actually were able to borrow more than their costs. They had cash to spare from the loans without even selling the property. Loans such as this are seldom made today; however, in some situations 100 percent loans and even greater loans are possible.

Suppose you have an option to buy a lot for $100,000, a contractor who will put up a building for $400,000 and a national tenant who has signed a long-term net lease for the premises to be built for $60,000 per year. Because of this lease, the property is really worth more than the $500,000 it would take to buy the lot and build the building. A lender might set a value of $800,000 on the property and agree to give you permanent financing of $550,000, which would mean a loan for $50,000 more than your total cost.

Assume that a seller is unwilling to sell with no downpayment or that the downpayment desired is more than you can pay. In this case you might be able to buy the building only and agree to rent the land from the owner on a long-term lease. You should be able to reduce the sales price by the land value, and the seller will usually like the idea and security of retaining title to the land. Owners who otherwise would not consider a low or no downpayment find this type of offer very tempting. As part of the purchase agreement you should try to negotiate an option to buy the land for cash within a stated period of time (as long a period as possible). The seller may require that the building be paid off when the option is exercised. This would mean that you would have to refinance the property to include land and building. If values increase through inflation, you will be able to refinance and buy the land. You end up in the same position as if you had purchased the land and building together.

While you might cringe at the thought of buying the improvements without the land and having only an option to buy the land, this is really no worse than having to make a balloon payment five to seven years after purchase. In this usual method of seller financing, you must refinance to pay the balloon payment. In buying the building without the land but with an option to buy the land, you are actually better off because you don't really have to refinance. If you fail to exercise the option, you still have the building and a lease. If you fail to obtain financing to pay a balloon payment, you would probably be foreclosed.

ADVANTAGES TO RENTING PROPERTY

When a property requires a great deal of personal property, such as furnished units, it is possible to rent the personal property rather than pay cash or come up with a large downpayment to finance it. An advantage of renting is that it is frequently easier to arrange than financing. In addition, rental payments for personal property used for business or investment are totally deductible for tax purposes. It is now possible to rent carpeting for office buildings and furniture for motels. Renting reduces the amount of money required to buy or build. Renting will, of course, increase your operational expenses. Generally, therefore, rentals should not be considered if there is already a negative cash flow.

SELLING ON A LOW OR NO DOWNPAYMENT

An owner can be induced to sell on a low or no downpayment by an offer to pay the full purchase price or even more. Often the seller doesn't really expect to get that much. You should couple the offer with a reduced interest rate. Today people are very tax conscious. A seller pays regular income tax on interest but gets capital gains treatment for the profit. By increasing the profit and reducing the interest rate, the seller might receive the same amount of money each month, but the tax consequences would be that the seller will be able to keep considerably more of it. An IRS agent told me that 7 percent interest would probably pass an audit but that a lower rate could cause the IRS to impute a higher rate. Check with a tax attorney or a CPA before you set up this kind of sale.

While such an arrangement might be attractive enough to influence a seller to sell with no or a low downpayment, it does create some tax problems for the buyer. The buyer's interest payments are deductible but payments on the principal are not. In this type of sale, you decrease the deductible portion of your payments because of the lower interest rate, and you increase the nondeductible portion by increasing the principal.

RAISING CASH

If you are buying an apartment building in which the tenants have made large security deposits or prepaid the last month's rent, you should realize that these deposits are turned over to the buyer at the closing of the transaction. They reduce the amount of cash you need to complete the transaction. If you don't have enough ready cash to complete a transaction, you should consider the following possibilities:

1. *Insurance policies.* If you have a whole life insurance policy, you can borrow up to your loan value. The loan value is usually shown on a table on the policy. An advantage of borrowing on your insurance is that loans are at a very low rate of interest. I borrowed on my GI policy to finance my honeymoon. I borrowed on it again to buy real estate. Since I am paying only 5 percent interest, I cannot imagine paying it back.
2. *Personal property.* You can borrow on your personal property such as furniture. This is a high-interest loan.
3. *Family loans.* Relatives are an excellent source of money. I recommend that family loans be in writing and bear interest. All payments should be by check. Avoid any possibility of a misunderstanding about the obligations and repayments. If you would rather not take money directly from relatives, you can borrow their credit instead. By having relatives cosign for you, you may be able to qualify for a loan.

Your ability to buy real estate depends directly on your credit. If you fail to meet obligations, you cannot expect others to trust you in dealings involving many thousands of dollars. In business, we measure a person by his or her past actions. You must therefore be zealous in protecting your credit, for in business your credit is your honor.

The natural tendency of every society in which property enjoys tolerable security is to increase in wealth.

—T. B. Macauley, 1835
Edinburgh Review

6

Partnerships, Syndicates and Investment Trusts

An often-quoted definition of a partnership is "two people getting together for a business or investment, one of which has the money and the other the experience, after which their positions become reversed." This cynical definition has unfortunately been true in too many cases. Many partnerships don't work out.

WHY SOME PARTNERSHIPS GO SOUR

Another old proverb is "A pig that has two owners is sure to die of hunger." Often what starts out as a close relationship can turn to discord. Often one partner feels he or she is contributing more than the other and therefore refuses to do any more. Whatever the reason, most partnerships are relatively short-lived, even when the business or investment is profitable. It also seems that the more partners there are, the more partnership problems there are.

Four students in an evening Master of Business Administration program asked my advice on a real estate investment. I told them of the problems of partnerships, but they said I didn't understand. The students were very close friends, almost family. They would not have any problems in that area but just wanted my opinion on a six-unit building in which they were interested.

The students purchased the building, which was well located but in bad shape. They were going to fix it up, get better tenants and sell it. Well, only two partners showed up to start work on the weekend after the purchase. One of the other two partners had a family affair he "had" to attend and the other one had to work at his job. The second weekend it was the same. It turned out that two partners carried the burden of work while the other two helped only on rare

47

occasions. One of these men was completely incapable of performing the simplest mechanical task.

During the renovating period, the property had a negative cash flow because the units were vacant for the renovation. In addition to the payments on the loans, materials had to be purchased. One of the partners who performed the large share of the work refused to contribute additional money for the payments. He argued that if everyone had worked as he had, the job would have been done; he would not pay for their laziness. The other three had to make the payments to avoid foreclosure. The building was put on the market for sale "as is" before the work was completed and while it was vacant. The four former friends sold the property and got their money back, but they now won't have anything to do with each other.

ADVANTAGES TO PARTNERSHIPS

Partnerships don't have to end this way. I have a partner in many of my investments. We get along great and have for years. We are good business friends, although socially we move in different circles. We have agreed to a division of responsibility and we stick to it. Our teamwork has been fun as well as profitable; our different backgrounds complement each other.

Partnership agreements need not be in writing to be enforceable; nevertheless, I recommend putting them in writing, as ours is. It is not so much a matter of trust as business. To avoid misunderstandings, we have written down our rights and duties. Our agreement is quite formal, and I believe having it in writing has helped our partnership to work.

A big advantage a partnership offers to an investor is courage. Many people will not move to invest alone but will invest with a partner. Another person who agrees that an investment is good reinforces a person's convictions. When it comes to investing their savings, most people lack strong confidence. Without the psychological crutch of a partner, many investors would not have made their first real estate investment. After several successful investments as a partner, investors frequently gain the confidence to make investments by themselves.

Another advantage of a partnership is that it can provide greater capital, thus allowing the investors to buy higher-quality investments. It also allows an investor who is running scared to invest with low liability.

Occasionally you will see a "partner wanted" ad. While the investment may be excellent, don't jump at it. A partnership is like a marriage; it must be carefully nurtured to succeed. It can either be a beautiful relationship or a living hell. Don't enter a partnership with a stranger.

You don't necessarily have to have money to make money in a partnership. I know of a hard-working young man who purchased a fixer-upper house with a partner who put up all the money. The young man provided the labor and when the house was later sold at a profit, the profit was split after the other party was repaid for his investment.

LIMITED PARTNERSHIPS

So far I have been discussing general partnerships. There is another type of partnership which is quite different—a limited partnership. A limited partner is an inactive partner who contributes only money to an investment. While in a general partnership a partner had unlimited personal liability for the partnership debts, in a limited partnership the limited partner's liability is limited to his or her investment. If the partnership fails, the limited partner is not personally liable to unpaid creditors. The limited partner has all of the advantages of an individual or general partner-owner, such as depreciation and other tax benefits. But the limited partner has none of the landlord's hassles. They are taken care of for him by a general partner.

In every limited partnership there must be one active or general partner. The general partner is personally liable for the partnership debts. To avoid this liability, the general partnership is often a corporation. Individual stockholders and officers of a corporation have no personal liability for corporate debts.

The general partner is the one who puts the deal together by locating a property to buy and the investors. For this and for actively managing the investment, the general partner is compensated. Sometimes compensation is a piece of the property or a percentage of the profit when the property is sold. There are many different compensation agreements for general partners. The success or failure of an investment usually hinges on the judgment and ability of its general partner.

I have a school teacher friend who became quite well off because of limited partnerships. This young man was a native and knew all the old-timers in an area where everyone seemed to be from someplace else. He had an excellent knowledge of the real estate and agriculture in the area. With a wife and three small children, he didn't have money to invest. He saw what he considered to be "steals" go by because he couldn't put together even a modest downpayment.

The young man heard of a ranch for sale and thought it was a terrific opportunity. He went to see the owner and the owner agreed verbally to give him a ten-day option to buy the property. This option was not legally enforceable because it was not in writing and no consideration was given for it. Nevertheless, this young man felt that it would be honored.

He contacted quite a few of his friends and acquaintances, including his doctor, dentist and attorney and had a meeting at his home. With maps of the area, he presented to them why it was a good investment. He told them about the depreciation possibilities on the citrus trees and why he felt that a quick resale for profit was possible if desired. The price of the ranch was $400,000 with a $50,000 downpayment required. The young man told his audience he wanted five investors as limited partners. Each would put up $15,000, which would give them some money for payments. The groves could be leased to another grower, but the property would still have a negative cash flow and the investors would each have to plan on coming up with another $5,000 every year. For acting as the general partner he asked for one-sixth of the investment to be paid out of profits after a sale. His share was not to be computed until all monies invested by the limited partners were repaid. Well, he found his five investors that night. Within a few months the property sold for $600,000.

The teacher found other properties, and his partners rolled over their profits into his new ventures. Several of those who failed to get into the first venture now wanted in. Friends of investors became interested as well. Once you have tasted success, investors tend to find you.

While this young teacher succeeded without a cash investment, limited partners are more willing to invest if the general partner has a cash position in the investment. Investors prefer the general partner to have a very positive interest in the success of the group.

This young man has quit his job teaching and spends all of his time on his partnership business. He recently told me that he believed he could raise $1,000,000 cash in an afternoon on the telephone from people who have made money with him in the past. Right now he is riding a wave of success, but not all limited partnerships are successful. In striving for great profits, limited partnerships are usually highly leveraged. That is, they are financed as much as possible. Sometimes an unexpected vacancy rate can make the difference between success and failure. Many people have lost their life savings when limited partnerships failed.

If you are interested in setting up a limited partnership for real estate investments, have an attorney draw up the papers.

SYNDICATES

An attorney can also advise you as to any state regulations concerning small syndicates. A syndicate is simply a real estate partnership in which the investors have limited liability.

I personally don't like to invest in syndicates or to set them up. I prefer to trust my money to my own knowledge and control. Also, I do not like the responsibility of worrying about other people's money, it makes me far too conservative in my actions.

Because of my personal feelings about these group investments, I lost out on the syndicate deal of a lifetime. Several professors at my college found a 400-acre parcel which could be purchased at $2,000 an acre. Smaller parcels in the area were selling at between $3,000 and $5,000 an acre. My colleagues purchased the parcel by forming a group of ten investors who each put down $12,000. One of the group was an active partner who took a larger share for his efforts.

Probably the most important element of an investment is timing, and in this case several large developments were announced in the vicinity of this parcel even before escrow closed. Within ninety days of closing their purchase, they had the property sold. They used a long escrow to get long-term capital gains. The net profit to each of the investors was $240,000 on a $12,000 investment, or a 2,000 percent profit in one year.

If someone wants you to invest in a syndicate or limited partnership, look at the track record of the general partners. Find out what else he or she has done in the past. Get the names of previous investors, and call them to verify profits and the relationship. Ask if they know of other investments the general partner has been involved in. The general partner might neglect to tell you of investments that didn't work out well.

REAL ESTATE INVESTMENT TRUSTS (REIT)

REITs are organized under federal law. There must be at least 100 members and at least 90 percent of the income must be distributed to the investors each year. The shares in the trust are freely transferable and for tax purposes are treated as a partnership rather than a corporation. A corporation is subject to double taxation in that the profit is taxed to the corporation and the remainder is again taxed to the individual stockholders if it is paid out as dividends. In a partnership, profit is simply taxed once to the partners. In a REIT only the earnings retained by the trust are taxed to the trust.

In the past there has been fraud in some REITs and syndicates. Property has been purchased from the organizers at exorbitant prices. In other cases property has been purchased and sold to generate brokerage fees for the organizers and not because of market or investor profit considerations. I would recommend that you check before you invest and that you stick with experienced organizers. Many of the organizers of Real Estate Investment Trusts started out working with small groups of their friends. Many have long records of success.

With partnerships, syndicates and trusts you really don't have to have money to make money in real estate. You just have to find people who do have money and who trust your judgment.

If you want to make money in real estate, find out where the people are going and get there first.

—*Will Rogers*

7

Locating Property

Once you have made the decision to invest in real estate and have some idea of what you want from a real estate investment, you face the task of locating property which meets your needs.

Looking for property can occupy as much time as you have available. There are many people who have retired from their career jobs who are now occupied full time in locating property for personal investment purposes.

USING REAL ESTATE BROKERS AND SALESPEOPLE

The easiest way to find property is through real estate professionals—the real estate brokers and salespeople who are active in your area. They know what is available and frequently what isn't available but could be. A knowledgeable real estate agent can also give you a good perspective on price and current market conditions. In a few hours an agent can often present many properties for consideration. What could have taken months might be accomplished in a few days or even hours. Many brokers belong to multiple listing services, so they have access not just to their own office listing but to the listings of many other offices as well.

In order to get the maximum benefit of a real estate agent's time and expertise, you should fully inform the agent as to how much cash or other assets you have available for a downpayment and for monthly payments. You may find some unimaginative real estate agents who are not interested in working with you if you can't make a substantial downpayment. This type of agent usually lacks the knowledge and imagination necessary to structure purchases with little or no downpayment.

In selecting real estate agents to help you, you should look for success. A successful agent is usually better informed as to the availability of property.

He or she will have the skills necessary to match your needs with appropriate property in a professional manner. If you feel an agent is not really working for you, don't hesitate to contact other agents. Many successful investors have developed a close working relationship with just one or two real estate agents whom they trust and respect. An agent who fully understands your needs and who is willing to expend his or her effort to meet those needs in an expeditious manner is a valuable asset.

You must keep in mind that, while the real estate agent may try to find property which meets your needs, in a normal sale transaction the agent represents the seller and not you, the buyer. Some agents will therefore try to sell you property unsuitable for your purposes. To some agents, earning a commission takes priority over serving customer needs.

WHY A THIRD PERSON CAN MAKE A DIFFERENCE

The seller normally pays the real estate commission. Therefore, it doesn't cost you money as a buyer to deal through a real estate agent. In fact, if you submit an offer which differs greatly in price or terms from what the owner is asking, a third person usually has a much greater chance of getting the offer accepted than you would have in dealing directly with the owner. Owners tend to be calmer and more objective when they are dealing through an agent. They are not as likely to let emotions affect their judgment.

Some time back my wife found a condominium she liked. I felt that the owner, who was selling it directly, was asking an unrealistically high price. I made an offer which was a little over 20 percent less than her asking price. The owner became indignant and refused to talk to me. Six months later I discovered that she had listed the condominium with a real estate broker at an even higher price, apparently to take care of the commission. I contacted the broker and presented the identical offer which had been refused months earlier. This time the broker was able to discuss my offer with the owner calmly and it was accepted.

BUYING THROUGH AN AGENT

There are times when you may want a real estate agent to represent you as the buyer. Suppose you desire a particular type of property and there is nothing available on the market. In that case, you might agree to pay the real estate agent a commission should the agent locate a property which you decide to purchase.

An advantage of paying the commission is that it makes many more properties available. Some properties are not really for sale and the owners will not give listings, but they will nevertheless consider offers.

The fact that you agree to pay a commission does not necessarily mean that more cash will be needed for the purchase. When the buyer is paying the commission, a seller can frequently be persuaded to reduce the price and downpayment requirements. In addition, many brokers are willing to accept notes secured by a second mortgage in lieu of cash.

BUYING WITHOUT AN AGENT

Besides real estate agents you should also let friends and acquaintances know what you are looking for. Many sales are made because a friend knows someone who is considering selling his or her property. In this manner many sales are made without property ever being officially on the market. You will probably want to conduct your own search for property. Owner for-sale advertisements or signs are sources to investigate.

Often owners try to sell without an agent because they feel they can save a commission. Occasionally an unsophisticated owner will not have a good idea of values and will ask a bargain price. Usually, however, if the property has been on the market for any period of time, the owner has been contacted by many real estate agents and will have a good idea of values.

Sometimes an owner will place an unrealistically high value on property. The price may be based on what the owner believes some other house sold for or on what a real estate agent said the property could bring. Unfortunately, some real estate agents will try to "buy a listing" by appealing to an owner's greed and promising a sale at an unrealistic price. When an owner is given this sort of misinformation, it becomes difficult to purchase the property at a fair price.

You should beware of the sophisticated seller who is looking for an unsophisticated buyer. These owners may attempt either to hide something detrimental about the property or to obtain a price much higher than the market will justify. They may use deceiving ads. I have come across some shrewd operators who posed as "rubes" in order to trick a buyer. I am on my guard when I deal directly with owners.

DECIDING ON LOCATION

Property in Other Places.   Beware of property which is being offered out of its local area. Generally, this property is overpriced or there is some other reason why it hasn't sold locally.

Usually you should avoid property outside the United States because of high risk. Political turmoil and outright government appropriation of your property is possible. This is especially true in the economically emerging nations.

Location Value of Property.   Experts say the three most important considerations in purchasing real estate are location, location and location. Property in desirable locations will show the greatest increase in value during inflationary periods. A well-located property is normally much easier to sell or borrow money on. The better the location, the lower the investment risk. A bargain price without location is generally not a bargain.

A duplex in a desirable area of your city might be available for $125,000, while a similar duplex in a less desirable location might be purchased for $100,000. It is conceivable that in five years the $125,000 duplex could be worth $180,000 while the bargain duplex at $100,000 might be worth only $125,000. In this hypothetical case you can see that the $125,000 duplex is the real bargain.

Factors in Location Value.   Historically, while real estate values generally go up, some individual parcels do decline in value. These are usually properties in locations which have become less desirable. You should be on the alert for signs of area deterioration, population shifts or changes in use. If an area is considering a rent control ordinance, you should realize that if such an ordinance is passed, values will be held down because income will be artificially depressed.

The local economy is an important aspect of location. A growing economy generally means appreciation, while a stagnant economy generally means that your real property investments will stagnate as well. One-industry towns or cities have a much higher risk than well-balanced, multiindustry areas. When Anaconda announced in 1980 that they were leaving Anaconda, Idaho, local values nosedived. Overnight, homeowners lost more than ten years' appreciation, and even then there were no buyers.

You should try to ascertain the major directional growth of a metropolitan area. Property in the growth pattern offers the greatest appreciation potential. Locations near golf courses, colleges, parks and other recreational or educational facilities seem to have much greater than average appreciation.

In many urban areas we are seeing a back-to-the-city movement. Many central city areas are being redeveloped. While these are high-risk investments, they also offer fantastic profit potential. Property on the periphery of the major business areas is most likely to be redeveloped.

Unless you have the temperament to be a slum landlord, I advise against buying ghetto property. Even though it can often be purchased with a very low or no downpayment, it will exact a toll from you in time and general peace of mind you may not be willing to pay.

BUYING AT THE RIGHT TIME

I have a friend who does nothing but buy new homes and condominiums which he resells, usually at a profit. His criterion for buying is the public acceptance of a project. When sales are greater than expected for a subdivision, my friend will wait until they are almost sold out, then buy several units. When a desirable project is completed, the resales are usually at least 10 percent above the original sale price.

My friend has another formula for really large projects being developed in phases. If the first phase sales are exceptionally good, he will buy several units before they are sold out. When a developer has exceptional sales on the first phase of a project, the developer can be expected to raise prices significantly for later phases of the project.

In many states you can tie up a house or condominium with a very low downpayment before the final approval is received for the subdivision. In these states it is possible to sell your "reservation" or, if your contract precludes this, a double escrow is usually possible. When you close the transaction, you actually buy and resell at the same closing. In a boom period in Orange County, California in the late 1970s, many people became rich tying up units with low downpayments and then selling their reservations to others.

FINDING A BARGAIN

You should not dismiss property from consideration because the asking price is more than you consider the value to be. You should keep in mind that the majority of real estate sales are made at prices lower than the property listed for. The only way you can find out if an owner will accept what you consider a reasonable offer is to make the offer.

As a prospective purchaser you should bear in mind that even offers which slash the owner's asking price usually provide the owner with a profit. The average seller has held his or her property more than five years. With inflation, chances are the asking price is considerably more than the owner paid for the property. Properties which have been vacant for long periods and on which owners have been making large mortgage payments are ideal candidates for a low offer. To purchase this type of property, you should have the means to make the payments and faith in your ability to find a qualified tenant. Out-of-the-area owners are also often more receptive to low offers than area owners would be.

Don't be concerned that a property is dirty or needs maintenance. This helps you as an informed buyer, since many other buyers would be turned off by such a property. When there is little competition to buy, a bargain is more likely. A house which needs painting and yard work might be available for $80,000, even though it would be worth $100,000 when properly maintained. You can buy a lot of paint and lawn seed for $20,000.

In a rapidly rising real estate market you should not be overly concerned about obtaining bargains; this is usually a seller's market. With few sellers and many prospective buyers, you should just try to buy in a good area at a reasonable price. You could conceivably spend a year trying to buy property at 15 percent below the market. However, while you were looking, the property may have increased in value 18 percent. The net effect in this instance of waiting for the bargain is that you would pay more. If you are looking for the super dream deal, chances are you will never make a purchase. You are better off looking for many opportunities where a reasonable profit is possible rather than the one get-rich-quick deal. When you find what you consider to be a reasonable deal, act. Chances are it won't last long.

The longer a property has been on the market without an offer, the greater the chance that a purchaser can obtain a bargain in price or terms. If an owner has recently placed his or her property on the market, very low offers are likely to be rejected. When a property has been for sale for a long period without buyer interest, any offer is likely to receive serious consideration. Ask your real estate agent which listings have been on the market for an unusually long time.

There will be some bargains available regardless of the real estate market. Personal problems, such as divorce, death and legal or business problems, can create situations in which the seller wants a quick sale. Such situations can result in bargain purchases.

A friend of mine called on a blind house-for-sale ad. When he saw the house, he realized it was beyond his pocketbook. The owner asked what he could afford to pay. My friend told the owner, who agreed to sell it providing the sale could be closed in two weeks. After the sale the owner was indicted for a felony and was believed to have left the country.

I was recently offered a builder's model home at a bargain price because the builder was in serious financial trouble. Because of other commitments, I could not purchase the property but I told a friend of the deal.

SOME TYPES OF BARGAINS

Headache Property. Headache property can frequently be purchased at excellent values. Examples include property with fire and building code violations. You should keep in mind that repair costs frequently exceed the initial estimates.

Another type of headache property is property which requires a great deal of management effort. This category includes rooming houses, older hotels, some furnished residential units and property in or adjoining slum areas. While these types of property often can be purchased at prices which allow an excellent return for the buyer, they are less likely to appreciate in value. Investing in this type of property requires a willingness to spend time and energy in management and maintenance. If you are willing to take the aggravation, the profit opportunity is there.

Auctions.   These can sometimes result in real bargains. Auctions can be held in cases of sheriff's sale, bankruptcy, tax sale, probate sale or government surplus property. While these sales usually are for cash, it does not mean that all cash is required. Financing can be arranged before you make any bid.

Tax Sale Property.   This is property usually sold from a legal description. The clerk in the county recorder's office will usually show you how to locate property from the legal descriptions. It takes time, but real bargains are often found in tax sales. There are investors who work full time checking out property to be sold for taxes. There are many reasons people fail to pay taxes on valuable property. In some cases the owner has died and the heirs don't even know of the ownership.

Besides tax sales, a good source for purchases are properties not yet lost for taxes but on which the taxes have been delinquent for some time. Often these properties can be purchased by paying nothing down and just getting caught up with the taxes.

Foreclosures.   Buying real estate prior to foreclosure offers an excellent opportunity in both price and terms. Often a property can be purchased by just taking over the back payments. The advantage to the owner is that he or she does not have the foreclosure on his or her credit record. Sometimes, as an inducement, a buyer allows the owner to remain in possession for several months without paying any rent.

If owners in a foreclosure feel they have a real equity, they will normally want something for it. In such cases, owners will frequently accept a second mortgage in lieu of cash. Of course, in buying property prior to foreclosure, you would be primarily interested in situations where the existing loans are assumable. If an existing loan is not assumable, you would either have to pay it off with cash or obtain new financing.

After foreclosure, property can frequently be purchased from the lender at very favorable terms. Conventional lenders don't want real estate; they want interest. Contact the local office of HUD (U. S. Department of Housing and Urban Development), and ask to be placed on the list to receive announcements of foreclosures. HUD will usually sell their foreclosures with low downpayments.

OTHER WAYS OF FINDING PROPERTY

In some counties the county takes title to property of welfare recipients and sells the property after the death of the recipient.

Lumber and mining companies often have surplus land which has been logged or mined. The property may have been purchased for the particular trees or minerals on it and it is now surplus. These firms usually don't need cash, so attractive prices and terms are possible. Years ago companies often let this property revert back for taxes.

Some investors check county records to see who owns property they are interested in. They then write the owners to ask what they would accept for their property. Other investors actually send offers to owners on many properties. These investors are like fishermen; they feel if they throw out enough lures, one is going to be accepted.

After you have searched for property you will develop a feel for value. You will actually be appraising property in an informal manner based on your experiences with comparable properties. The knowledge of value you acquire will enable you to evaluate various purchase possibilities and will help you with your next step—analyzing property.

Every man who invests in well-selected real estate in a growing section of a prosperous community adopts the surest method of becoming independent, for real estate is the basis of wealth.

—Theodore Roosevelt

8

Analyzing Property

Don't count on a broker to tell you what you should buy. The broker generally represents the owner, who wants a sale at the best price and terms possible. Brokers are likely to be more interested in a sale than in what is right for you. Since you are the one putting up the money or accepting financial obligations, purchase decisions must be yours, based on your understanding of the property, the area and the economy.

THREE STAGES OF LOCATION VALUE

The first thing to consider for any purchase is location. Property tends to go through the three distinct stages of integration, equilibrium and disintegration. During integration the area is being developed. Early users often determine the character of future development. After being developed, an area generally goes through an equilibrium stage in which the character and use of the area remain relatively unchanged. Finally, the area will start to disintegrate or go downhill. It will become less desirable. Occasionally, an area is rescued and is revitalized from this stage.

These three stages of development hold true for individual properties as well as areas. They illustrate the principle of change, which means that use and values do not remain constant; change must always be expected.

DETERMINING VALUE

To find what stage a property is in, check the area. What is happening? You should consider what has happened to an area in the last year, the last five years and the last ten years. The changes which have taken place will give you an excellent indication of what will happen to the area in the future. The study of trends and changes is invaluable in deciding when and what to purchase, as well as when to sell.

Signs of Value.   Positive signs would be low vacancy factors, evidence of remodeling or expansion of existing structures or the replacement of existing buildings with new structures. In areas where commercial tenants are doing well, there will be few changes in businesses or ownerships. On the other hand, a high turnover in a location, as well as frequent changes in ownership, normally indicates marginal or loss operations. When people in an area are not doing well economically, maintenance often gets deferred. Because of rent collection problems, owners also tend to reduce expenditures to a minimum.

Other negative signs are a decrease in retail volume and a decrease in owner-occupied housing. Property tends to filter down to lower economic groups. Signs of this occurring could mean a lowering of values. An increasing crime rate is often accompanied by higher fire insurance rates for an area. These are also unfavorable indicators of values dropping. Conversions of large homes to apartments generally are a negative indicator. Abandoned buildings or unrepaired fire-gutted buildings usually indicate very severe problems for an area.

Demographics.   Such factors as income, age, family size, ethnic background and even religion can affect spending habits of the residents, which in turn has a bearing on commercial values.

Directional Growth.   New factories, golf courses, schools and so forth will tend to raise values in nearby areas. In most urban centers the best residential growth tends to be in a few areas. Generally, schools, parks and golf courses are very positive indicators of the direction of increased residential value.

In the same respect, blight is contagious. In what direction are blighted areas growing? Because of natural or artificial barriers, blight is often channeled in specific directions. You should consider the fact that the existence of present or former chemical dumps in an area would adversely affect value. Also, the presence of an atomic energy plant or even a large chemical plant can reduce values and might affect them more radically in the future.

Other Factors.   As to residential property, you should consider the location in relationship to jobs, public transportation, freeways, schools, shopping and recreational facilities. Commercial property is also affected by transportation, traffic count, population within the purchasing area of the property as well as its purchasing power and purchasing habits. Industrial property is concerned with location in relationship to a labor supply as well as transportation and availability of utilities.

Principles of Progression and Regression.   Generally, it is best to buy the least expensive property in a good area. The value of the other property will actually pull the value of your property up. This is known as the principle of progression.

The opposite is the principle of regression. It is not a wise investment to have the most valuable property in an area of lower-valued properties. The surrounding lower values will tend to pull the value of your property down. We can understand these principles if we consider a builder who builds a $250,000 home in an area of $100,000 homes. The lower values in the area would make the property difficult to sell at that price. If the house had been built in an area of $500,000 homes, it would probably be readily saleable even at a higher price.

ZONING

After evaluating the area, you should consider the zoning of the specific property. Will it allow the present or contemplated use? Is the zoning in the area consistent with the zoning of this particular parcel?

Look for evidence of down-zoning. Down-zoning is a change in zoning to more restrictive uses, such as a change from commercial to residential zoning. A number of instances of down-zoning in an area might indicate that other property might also be down-zoned. If an undeveloped property were down-zoned to a more restrictive use, it would tend to lower the value of the parcel.

It is also possible for zoning to be changed to make property more productive. As an example, a single-family home zoned for residential use could materially increase in value if it is rezoned for offices. You should therefore consider area zoning as well as individual property zoning, as area zoning patterns can affect future zoning changes. Many people have more than doubled the value of their properties by simply applying for and receiving zoning changes. The feasibility of rezoning to a more productive use makes a property much more attractive to an investor.

Just because a vacant property may be zoned for a particular number of units does not mean that number of units can be built on the parcel. When minimum square footages of each unit, parking requirements, height and side yard limits are all considered, it might be physically impossible to build the number of units allowed by the zoning.

Frequently, properties have nonconforming uses. The current use could have preceded the zoning. In these cases the use is allowed to continue but should it cease for some reason, the use cannot be started again. Generally, you can expect a property with a nonconforming use to have a lower value than if the use was consistent with the zoning.

Zoning Violations.   Some property has been used for years in violation of the zoning. Just because someone else got away with a zoning violation in the past does not mean that you will be able to do so in the future. For example, in the past many people remodeled to create a separate apartment for relatives, such as a mother-in-law unit. Later owners may have rented the extra unit in violation of the zoning.

If a unit has been remodeled for a change in use, such as an apartment split into more units or a large house broken up into apartments, you should be concerned with the zoning as well as with whether or not the work was accomplished with a building permit. Many people have bootlegged units. If units contrary to either the building codes or zoning are discovered, the result could be an order to tear out the work.

Abatements.   Should the use of a unit create noise or odors, that use could be stopped by an abatement order. The use, while lawful, could interfere with the rights of others to enjoy their property, in which case it could be considered a nuisance.

I know of a productive stone quarry which existed in an isolated area for years. When subdivisions built up in the area, the local government successfully brought an action to abate the nuisance. Because of the noise from the operation itself and the many heavy trucks, the use was considered a nuisance in the residential community.

COVENANTS, CONDITIONS AND RESTRICTIONS

Besides zoning, as a purchaser you should consider covenants, conditions and restrictions. These CC&Rs are private restrictions on the use of a property placed on property by a subdivider or by agreement of all the property owners subject to them. The restrictions may apply to use, size, height, building setbacks, architectural styles and even such things as colors. Even though zoning may allow a use, if the use violates the CC&Rs it would be possible for any other person subject to the same CC&Rs to obtain an injunction prohibiting the intended use. When CC&Rs and zoning disagree, whichever is more restrictive as to use would govern. Since the CC&Rs are recorded, they are available. A title company can obtain a copy for you.

SEWERS, WATER, ELECTRICITY AND NATURAL GAS

If you are buying undeveloped land, you will want to have information as to the availability of sewers, water, electricity and natural gas. Some utilities can be relatively close to a property, but the cost to bring them out to the property can be excessive if the property is prematurely developed.

If a sewer is not available but septic systems are allowed, you would want to know if the property can pass a percolation test. If it cannot, a building permit would not be issued. Many people have invested their savings in land which cannot be developed because of poor percolation. Percolation is a problem where the water table is close to the surface or where there is a great deal of clay.

Recently, a young man purchased three lakefront lots at a very good price. The lots were served by sewer and water and were at the end of a street which sloped to the lake. The buyer did almost everything right: he cleared the lots of brush so the view was opened, added sand fill where needed and generally made the lots very attractive. He intended to build his own home on one lot and sell the others. When the young man applied for his building permit, he discovered that he had to install a sewage lift station costing $18,000.

Check with the building department prior to purchase to avoid unpleasant surprises.

Just because a natural gas line is in place does not mean it is available for use. In some areas of the country utility companies are not taking on new customers because they are afraid they might not be able to supply their needs.

FACTORS LIMITING BUILDING GROWTH

Some communities are limiting the number of building permits issued. Schools, police and fire protection must be supplied to new residents and the communities feel they cannot cope with unrestricted growth. The purchase of land in such an area could be a gamble. If the restrictions remain, you can expect little appreciation for a long period of time. On the other hand, an investment in a developed property in a community which limits growth could have great appreciation. If there is a demand, the governmental restrictions on supply will work to raise values. The local building inspector will be able to tell you if there are any current or planned limitations on the number of building permits issued.

Some land has a compaction problem, which means that the land cannot properly support structures. Usually this would be land reclaimed by drainage or filled land. In some cases expensive pilings must be driven down to support a structure. Excessive construction costs will reduce value. If you feel that a parcel of land may not be able to support a structure, hire a civil engineer to check the property. If you are buying undeveloped land, I strongly recommend that you actually walk the boundaries of the land. If it is a large piece, you should also walk through the parcel so you fully understand its topography. Frequently, problems such as drainage will be discovered by such a walk. A little time spent can save you from a mistake.

DRAINAGE

Drainage is an important factor on raw land.

I recently volunteered to help find a new location for a workshop for retarded citizens. I found a location which appeared excellent and the price seemed extremely low. While the fact was not visible from the ground, I discovered by checking a topographic map that the property was in the center of a natural drainage area. Further checking with local residents revealed that the roads in the vicinity of the parcel and most of the parcel itself had been under as much as two feet of water on several occasions in the past twenty years.

I have learned that it pays to knock on doors and ask questions. Some communities will actually deny a building permit for a property in an area prone to floods.

ROADS

Roads which show on maps as nice straight lines can in reality be no more than a pair of tire ruts in the earth. What appears to be a public road to a property could very well be a private road over which you would not have rights. You can check with the county department of roads about a specific road. Undeveloped property on a major road, or on what looks like it could be a major route, can show dramatic appreciation. Roads which lie on section lines—government survey lines located every mile—often develop as major roads. Generally, land fronting on a section line road sells at a premium to investors.

About five years ago I was offered eight acres of land for $30,000. I didn't think the road the parcel was on would ever be a major traffic artery or that the land would be desirable to others. The road developed as a major artery and the parcel next to the one I was offered recently sold for $50,000 per acre. This would have been more than a 1200 percent profit if I had acted. At the time the parcel was offered to me the state highway department had extensive plans for widening the road and diverting other traffic to it. I had not bothered to check with them.

Decisions not to buy as well as to buy should be made based on available information. A phone call to the county or state highway department is now a must for me whenever I am interested in any highway frontage property.

VEHICULAR AND PEDESTRIAN TRAFFIC

For commercial property, the traffic count, the hours of peak vehicle traffic, traffic speed and foot traffic all affect value. If traffic is primarily during relatively short periods in the morning and late afternoon, then the property is probably on a route to a major employment area. Most of these drivers are in a hurry to and from work. Property on such a route would not be as valuable for commercial purposes as a location with the same traffic count spread over a longer period of the business day.

Traffic moving on a street at fifty miles per hour is much more difficult to stop than that moving at twenty-five miles per hour. Slower traffic is more desirable for retail businesses. Foot traffic is of course important for retail locations with window displays. An ideal location for foot traffic is between two major stores.

Parking is extremely important today for commercial, industrial and even residential properties.

I know of a 12,000-square-foot commercial building for sale. It's in a congested area and has only ten parking spaces. I own a much older building in the same general area. The street my building is on has half the traffic count of the other building. In addition, the building I own is quite plain, while the building up for sale is very deluxe. Nevertheless, my building gets almost twice the rent per square foot as the other structure. I believe the difference is that I have over fifty parking spaces in a large paved lot readily accessible from two streets.

PROPERTY SHAPE

Even the shape of a parcel can affect its value. A triangular lot will generally sell for less than a rectangular parcel since the rectangular parcel can be developed for greater utilization of the lot at a lower price.

People today like ranch homes which spread across the face of the lot and show all the world how large the owner's home is. Therefore, wide residential lots are more valuable than narrow deep lots having the same total square footage.

UTILITIES

In analyzing developed property you should be very concerned about whether the owner pays utilities and whether the utility rate increases are passed on to the tenant. In the past few years Consumer Price Index increases have not been sufficient to cover actual utility increases. Many properties operate at losses because they are leased to tenants who are not obligated to cover these increases. When you check on a property, you will be given figures on utility costs. You should ask to see actual utility bills, not just figures. Make your own estimate of current and anticipated utility costs based on the actual utility consumption in the past. Some owners will give you the average of several years' bills. These figures are meaningless since rates have been increasing. The older bills will tend to make the figures look more reasonable. The only thing that is meaningful in old bills is the actual cubic feet of gas, gallons of oil and kilowatts of electricity used. Be careful: some sellers might neglect to tell you that the annual figures include a period of several months when the premises were not occupied. To avoid surprises, I recommend that you estimate that utility costs will increase 15 to 20 percent annually for at least the next five years.

INSULATION

If a building has poor insulation, you should consider whether the costs of added insulation would result in savings. The federal tax credits for insulation should be considered. In addition, some states also offer credits or tax deductions. As a rule of thumb, I make an improvement if increased revenues or cost reductions will offset the cost of the improvement in six years. Of course, improvements can be depreciated for tax purposes.

Today I would think twice about structures with the poured-in foam insulation of the type which gives out formaldehyde fumes. From early reports, I believe many of these structures may have to be ripped open and the insulation removed due to health hazards. Keep in mind that consumers are becoming fearful about possible cancer as well as other reactions from chemical exposure.

Exotic energy sources such as solar heat in most areas are not economically feasible. While free energy sounds good, the cost to use the free energy of nature has kept its use generally uneconomical.

CHECKING OUT RENT COSTS

If a property is rented, you should analyze the rent. How does it compare to rentals charged for similar property in the area? While a property might be rented at a rate in excess of the rental rates for similar properties, you can usually expect such a property to have a much higher vacancy rate than properties rented at a more competitive rate.

The rent schedules owners provide cannot always be believed. An owner may fail to inform you that one tenant has a reduced rent for some management duties. One owner neglected to tell me that he had just notified the tenants of the new higher rent schedule and that three of his twelve tenants had thereupon given him notice. He just told me that this was his current rent schedule and informed me how long each tenant had been there. From the facts given, it looked good. While the facts were all true, the intent was to deceive.

Rent Concessions.   It is possible to rent property at a rate far above going rental rates by giving concessions. As an example, while a comparable apartment might rent for $250 per month, an owner might be able to get a tenant to move in on a one-year lease at $300 per month by giving the tenant the first two months' rent free. The tenant is really paying the same rent ($3,000) for one year as would have been paid in twelve months at $250. A buyer who expected the $300 rate to continue would find that tenants would move out or demand another rent concession prior to renewing their leases.

I check rentals with the tenants themselves. I want to verify rents, find out how long the present rental rate has been in effect and whether any concessions were given to rent the unit.

Checking Owner's Tax Returns.   Some prospective buyers want to see the owner's tax returns for the previous two or three years. These will show rental trends as well as trends in expenses. It is excellent information for helping with projections of income and expenses.

Vacancies.   Even though a particular building is fully rented, you should realistically consider a vacancy factor. By checking with a local apartment owners' organizations or with large property management firms, you can get a good idea of the vacancy rate for the area. Tenants do move, and even when units are quickly rented, there is usually a period when rent is not collected. The period can be from a few days to several months. In addition, sooner or later you will have a tenant who moves out owing money which will never be collected. You cannot realistically expect 100 percent occupancy and 100 percent collections.

GETTING THE RIGHT INFORMATION ON RENTALS

When inquiring about a property, be on the alert for terms such as *scheduled rents*. This does not mean that the rents are actually being collected. Another term frequently used is *broker's net income*. This is not a net figure, as it does not consider either a vacancy factor or any collection loss. It represents, the ideal, not the actual, situation.

In situations where there is not a good rental history, such as in the case of new buildings, real estate agents prepare a *pro forma statement*. This is not a statement of current income or expenses but rather an estimate as to what they will be. Brokers, in preparing these statements, tend to be overly optimistic. The figures given should not be accepted without your own independent analysis. I have seldom seen a pro forma statement in which the actual income exceeded what was estimated or in which expenses were less than contemplated. If I doubt figures provided by an owner, I will insist they be verified by tax returns. An owner will not declare income greater than actually received or expenses less than actually occurred when taxes are involved.

LOW RENTALS

There are actually many instances when rents are too low. Sometimes an owner has become a friend of the tenants and hesitates to increase rents. Other times it is simply poor management. Often when property is held in an estate there is no real incentive for the administrator to increase rents. The administrator is more concerned with avoiding problems. Sometimes out-of-the-area owners are unaware of the rental potential of their properties. I know one commercial tenant who scared the out-of-state landlord into giving an extremely low rent with the threat of leaving, despite the fact that the property was highly rentable. In analyzing a property's income, you should consider the feasible income and not necessarily what is actually received. Income which is frequently overlooked is parking revenues and receipts from coin-operated laundry equipment.

INSURANCE COSTS

When analyzing insurance costs, you might want to obtain a copy of the current policy to determine coverage and costs. Often an owner's coverage is more in relation to the price the owner paid than to the current value. This means coverage may be inadequate and proper coverage would increase the insurance costs far beyond the figure shown.

Coverage is very important. You should consider smoke and water damage as well as fire and lightning. Losses from vandalism and from nature should be considered. If a property has plate glass windows, you should consider coverage. Rental interruption insurance might be a consideration. It reimburses the owner for rent loss because of damage and destruction. If personal property is included with the property, it should also be covered. In this lawsuit-happy world it is essential that you carry substantial liability coverage. Flood and earthquake insurance should also be considered in areas prone to either of these. Your actual insurance costs could end up several times higher than the present owner's costs.

Tax figures provided by the owner are usually of little value in predicting your own tax obligations. Property is usually reassessed when sold. The new assessment is likely to be materially higher than the figure used for the previous owner. A better estimate of taxes can be based on the recent reassessment of similar properties.

SPECIAL PURPOSE BUILDINGS

If a tenant leaves a special purpose building, it could be vacant for a long time. Some special buildings have had vacancy periods measured in years rather than months.

I know of a family who built a large cold-storage building in a small town. They built it for a food processor who had been in business for many years. Less than one year after the building was completed, the parent corporation of the food processor went into bankruptcy. The building is still vacant more than three years later. Consider carefully the higher risks associated with investing in special purpose buildings.

ASSESSING PHYSICAL STRUCTURE

Paint.   In checking a structure, don't let a coat of paint fool you. Cosmetic repairs can hide serious problems. In the same manner, remember that paint is cheap; don't let the need of paint negatively affect your purchase decisions.

Electrical Wiring.   Many older buildings are not wired adequately for today's living.

A number of years ago I failed to properly check a structure when I purchased a large older home which appeared in excellent condition. I thought the price was within a reasonable price range as a home, but I envisioned a possible zoning change. The house was on a major street with some spot zoning of commercial property in the next block and completely commercial zoning several blocks away. As a commercial lot, the property would be worth several times what I had paid. The house had been occupied for many years by an elderly couple. Walls were either attractively painted or papered. The hardwood floors gleamed. The couple had beautiful furniture which made the old house look really great.

I didn't bother to check the electrical service until after I had purchased the property. I found out then that the house had not been rewired since it was built in the 1890s. There were no electrical outlets in the bedrooms, just ceiling lights. There were a total of three electrical outlets on the first floor and one on the second floor. From the neighbors I learned that the couple had used extension cords throughout the house, which had not been evident when I viewed the property. I tried to rezone the property but met stiff opposition from the neighbors, who did not want to see the character of the area changed. I couldn't blame them as the rezoning could adversely affect their quality of life, although it would also greatly increase the value of their own property.

Having failed at my rezoning, I decided to sell the property. Unlike the couple who sold me the house, I did not want to hide any defects in selling the property. Also, I didn't want to invest over $2,000 to rewire the house. I decided to capitalize on its faults and placed the following ad in the local newspaper:

ELECTRICIAN'S DREAM HOUSE
Actually the 19th-century wiring in this two-story coloni-al home belongs in a museum. If you know your AC from your DC, this property is for you. The house is set back from the street on a spacious lawn. The garage was originally a carriage house and has a storeroom, hobby room or studio above. The house is spic and span and ready to move into, but bring your own electricity.

Honesty pays. I sold the property to an electrical contractor who was also an antique buff, but I learned a lesson: don't assume; check it out.

Roofing. Check the roof, especially if it is flat. Flat roofs have a shorter life and need more frequent repairs than pitched roofs. Look for discolored water spots on the ceilings, which indicate leaks. If the roof has a pitched area and a flat area, the likely place for leaks is where these areas join. If an owner indicates a new roof was put on or that a roof was repaired, ask who did the work. Check with the roofer as to the condition of the roof. A roofer will give you an honest assessment, since misinformation will only alienate you as far as future work is concerned.

Plumbing. Copper plumbing will generally be in good shape. Pipes likely to cause you problems are iron or galvanized pipes. Test all faucets. Poor water flow could indicate a build-up of lime deposits in the pipes. Discoloration of water could indicate some iron pipes.

Property Age.   When you check the plumbing in a building, you can also check its age. Until very recently, all toilet tanks had the date of manufacture stamped inside the tank. Ordinarily, a tank is installed within six months of manufacture. Unless the fixtures were updated during remodeling, this date gives a fairly accurate age of a property.

Another way to determine age is to check the walls around the water heater and furnace. Building inspectors usually nail their approvals in these areas. Often the approvals say "Do not remove." People generally follow instructions, so these original construction approvals are often found on buildings being torn down. A more accurate way to ascertain the age of a building is to check with the tax assessor's office. You can find the first year the improvements were taxed. I don't bother asking real estate agents how old a building is since I have never had a real estate agent give an accurate estimate. Very often the age he or she quotes falls far short of the actual age of the structure.

Basements.   In checking a property with a basement, you should look for water lines on the basement walls. These lines indicate previous flooding or sewer backup problems. Also check the foundation or basement for cracks. They indicate settling but are not usually serious. You can, however, make a fuss over small cracks, which will place an owner on the defensive and help your bargaining position.

Foundations.   You should check the foundation for earthen tunnels running up to the wood. Be particularly alert in areas where the ground level is close to the wood. If the tunnels have been removed, you will see marks which look like a line on a map indicating a road that is not quite straight. If you find indications of these lines, then the structure has or had termites. You should insist on or arrange a termite inspection. Again, while the damage may only be slight, the presence of termites places you in an excellent bargaining position. Be sure you know the extent of the damage before you give an offer on a property.

OTHER ITEMS TO CHECK

You should also check furnaces and air conditioners. Don't assume that everything is working properly. If a home has pocket doors which glide into the wall, check them out. Frequently they don't work properly and repairs can be costly. If a house has a crawl space, you can check for dry rot. Checking requires a pocket knife, a flashlight and some very old clothes. In older properties you should check flooring around plumbing fixtures for rot. One sign of a problem is a loose tile.

If I see neighbors outside, I will stop and talk with them. I can usually find out if the property or the neighborhood has any problems of which I am not aware.

Bugs are not usually a problem as they can be exterminated. They can be an ally to you because the presence of bugs is a bargaining point in your favor. A roach running across a floor can knock several thousand dollars off a purchase price.

If repairs are necessary, get estimates. To be realistic, increase the average estimate by 50 percent: that is what you can expect to pay. As repairs progress, it is common to discover additional work which must be done.

EVALUATING TENANTS

Just as we evaluate a building, we can also evaluate tenants. Even though a tenant might be on a long-term lease or on only a month-to-month lease, we can predict whether or not the tenant will remain. This is of particular importance in special use structures. The tenant's financial strength is of course important. A Dunn and Bradstreet report will show the tenant's financial rating. The location of other businesses of the same type as the tenant's are also indications. If similar businesses have been moving out of the area, it is a negative indicator as to your present tenant. The nature and extent of tenant improvements and planned improvements can be strong indicators of a tenant's intent. You should consider what you would do if the present tenant left.

PROFESSIONAL APPRAISALS

We are now ready to determine what a property is worth. What a previous owner paid does not determine value. Don't worry that the price you offer is far more than the owner paid. On the other hand, don't feel you must offer at least what the owner paid. Values are based on what willing buyers will pay to willing sellers at the present time, not at some time in the past.

A quick way to get a feel for value is to have a lender appraise the property for a loan. A lender's appraisal will generally be conservative. If you don't feel qualified to make a good judgment as to value, I recommend you hire a fee appraiser. Don't just ask the broker to tell you what the property is worth; get an independent appraisal by an expert. Its cost can save you worry, heartache and a financial mistake. I recommend that you look for a professional appraiser who has one or more of the following designations:

MAI—This designation stands for Member of the Appraisers Institute of the American Institute of Real Estate Appraisers, an affiliate organization of the National Association of Realtors. The MAI designation is considered by many professionals to be the highest professional designation in the appraisal field. It requires competence in both residential and nonresidential appraisal.

RM—This identifies a Residential Member of the American Institute of Real Estate Appraisers. It requires demonstrated expertise in residential appraising.

SRA—This stands for Senior Residential Appraiser, a designation of the Society of Real Estate Appraisers. While the organizations themselves probably would not agree, I consider it comparable to the RM designation.

SRPA—The Senior Real Property Appraiser designation of the Society of Real Estate Appraisers is given for competence in income and residential appraisal.

SREA—The Senior Real Estate Analyst designation is given by the Society of Real Estate Appraisal for competence in all types of real property appraisal. It is the highest designation of the Society of Real Estate Appraisers.

There are several other organizations that also give professional designations; however, I recommend only appraisers with professional designations from the American Institute of Real Estate Appraisers or the Society of Real Estate Appraisers.

APPRAISAL METHODS

Everyone who deals in real estate should have a basic understanding of the following methods of appraisal:

Market Comparison Method.   This is the easiest appraisal method to learn and is used by most people when they buy property. They simply compare a property to other properties. When people say a price is too high, what they usually mean is that the price is higher than the price of a substitute property providing similar benefits of ownership. Using this method, we balance out amenities. For example, while one house has a two-car garage, a comparable house might have only a carport but also a fireplace. The homes might balance out, or you might feel that one is worth a particular dollar amount more than the other. We consider tenants, lease terms and financing in comparing properties. By checking the market, the average investor can get a very good feel for value based on comparables.

Replacement Cost Method.   This method of appraisal is generally used on new structures or on service-type buildings such as public libraries where there are no comparables. Using the replacement cost approach to value, we determine what it would cost to build a similar structure today that provides similar benefits. We can then deduct the accrued depreciation (reduction in value caused by use and age). To this figure the value of the land is then added. The land value can be estimated by the market comparison method.

$$
\begin{aligned}
&\underline{\hspace{2cm}} \text{ cost to build today} \\
\text{minus} - &\underline{\hspace{2cm}} \text{ accrued depreciation} \\
\text{plus} + &\underline{\hspace{2cm}} \text{ land value} \\
\text{equals} = &\underline{\hspace{2cm}} \text{ value of the property}
\end{aligned}
$$

The problem with this method of appraisal is that it is frequently difficult to determine the amount of the accrued depreciation.

Income Method. This method is used for income property. First the net income is ascertained. In determining net, we deduct all expenses from the gross income. The only expenses not deducted are interest expense and payments on the principal. This net is then divided by a capitalization rate. There are various methods to arrive at the rate, but it is really just the rate of return which an investor wants on an investment of this particular type. The greater the risk, the greater the rate of return an investor desires.

$$
\text{rate} \sqrt{\text{net}} = \text{value}
$$

Gross Multiplier. This is actually not a true appraisal method. It is only a way to get a ball-park figure. Assume that for a particular type of property investors are currently paying prices equal to nine times the annual gross receipts. Multiply the gross times nine, and if the price asked was equal to or less than this amount, then you would want to investigate further. Since the gross multiplier does not consider unusual expenses, it can be dangerous as an appraisal tool. I consider gross multiplier figures to be of little or no value to a serious investor.

In years past, investors talked about cash-on-cash return, or the actual cash returned on the cash investment. They also talked about cash throw-off, which is simply disposable cash income or net spendable income. Things have changed radically in the last few years. Only in a few areas of the country can quality properties be found which produce any disposable cash returns unless huge downpayments are made. Today investors get excited over a good break-even investment. In fact, negative cash-flow investments which investors would have laughed at a few years ago are snapped up today if the depreciation benefits offset the negative cash flow.

The income approach to value no longer works. The market place has increased values because of inflation. The basic economic principles of supply and demand underlie all evaluation. A market in which there are many willing buyers with few sellers means rising prices. The price you will pay today is determined by the market place. The market place reacts to what is anticipated. Future inflation is generally anticipated, which means properties will appreciate in value. Current rents will rise in the future. Today's negative cash flows are expected to turn to healthy positive cash flows within a few years. If you believe that inflation will continue, you can expect a general increase in real estate valuations. What today might seem a horrendous price could very well be tomorrow's bargain.

When you have found a property which meets your needs and you have a feel for its value, you are now ready for the next step—your offer to purchase.

Every man by nature has the right to possess property as his own. This is one of the chief points of distinction between man and the lower animals.
—*Pope Leo XIII, 1891*

9

Your Offer to Purchase

All right, you have found a property you are interested in and want to make an offer. First of all you should realize that a "firm" price is seldom firm. Some bargaining is usually possible. Even when a seller refuses to reduce a price, he or she will frequently negotiate on downpayment or interest rates.

KNOWING WHAT THE SELLER PAID

Before you prepare an offer, it helps if you know what the seller has invested in the property. By knowing when the seller purchased the property, you should be able to get a fairly good idea of what the seller paid. By telling neighbors that you are interested in purchasing in the area, you can lead up to the property and find out when the present owner purchased it.

It is important to know what the seller paid because a seller is unlikely to accept a major price cut which results in a loss. Owners are more likely to accept a price cut when it cuts only profit. If an owner wants $100,000 for a home and receives an offer of $75,000, the offer might be accepted if the owner had paid only $40,000. If the owner had recently purchased the property for $90,000, there is much less chance of the offer being accepted. Therefore, in a buyer's market, bargains are more likely from sellers who have owned property for a number of years. Owners are also more willing to finance the buyer when they are primarily financing profit dollars.

If a property has recently been placed on the market, a substantial price reduction is likely to be rejected. However, when a property has been on the market for a long time without any offers, even a very low offer will usually receive favorable consideration. I recently purchased a condominium for $55,000 when the units had sold new for $71,900. The unit had been on the market for a year and the owner wanted to return to the East.

77

When making an offer, you should keep in mind that while $29,900 psychologically will seem to you to be much lower than $30,000, it will appear much lower to the seller as well. It could be well worth it to round off the price offered.

PROBLEM PROPERTIES

Often problem properties can be purchased at attractive prices and terms. When a property has problems such as vacancies or health or building code violations, any offer may look good to an owner. If a property has developed a negative cash flow and the owner must pay a significant sum each month to keep the property, what would otherwise be an unacceptable offer just might be accepted.

I liked an old drive-in restaurant which had been closed for many years. It was on a 100-by-500 foot highway lot near a small resort city. One problem with the lot was that it would not perc test. This means that the soil could not support a septic system, so any user would have to use a holding tank for sewage and have it pumped out regularly. While a city sewer line was within half a mile, more development would be necessary before it would be extended. The sewer problem was the reason the lot had not sold. If the property had a sewer, a value of $70,000 would not be excessive. As it was, the property had been listed for sale at $35,000 for several years without any buyers. I didn't think this price was really out of line, but I felt that a significantly lower offer might be accepted because of the problems and the length of time it had been on the market. The building of 800 square feet was of concrete block and in good repair. The windows had all been boarded up since the drive-in closed. I felt that I could rent the property for a number of uses such as construction office and yard, used car or implement dealer or real estate office. In fact, I had a tentative tenant lined up. I came in with my offer after several weeks of consideration. I was too late. My offer of $24,000 was presented just one day after the seller had accepted an offer of $13,500. You never know what will be accepted until you test the seller with an offer.

BUYER'S AND SELLER'S MARKETS

There are times and situations when bargains are available in both prices and terms. In a buyer's market, where there are few buyers and many sellers, bargains are possible. There are always some sellers who for some reason must sell quickly. While a very low offer in a normal market might be rejected immediately, in a buyer's market the below-market offer will usually either be accepted or the seller will come back with a counter offer. When few offers are being made, an outright rejection of offers is unlikely.

In a seller's market, you will have to look for sellers who will carry paper. In a buyer's market this is less likely to be a problem, since sellers then seldom get what they want. Owners who want all cash find that they have to carry paper if they want a sale. The better the financial condition of the seller, the greater the possibility that the seller will carry paper.

Seller motivation will affect your offer. The more information you have on the seller, the stronger may be your bargaining position. You should keep in mind that while you don't have to buy a particular property, the seller may have to sell. This can put you in the proverbial catbird seat. You are the one bargaining from a position of strength.

OBTAINING FAVORABLE TERMS IN A SELLER'S MARKET

While bargains in price are seldom available in a seller's market, a purchaser can nevertheless often obtain favorable terms equivalent to a bargain price. For example, assume the going mortgage rate is 12 percent. If savings and loan institutions are paying depositors 8 percent, an owner might be persuaded to carry the paper on the transaction at 9 percent interest if the full asking price is paid. If the loan were $100,000 at 9 percent, the monthly payment on a twenty-year amortized loan would be $899.73. This amount at a 12 percent rate would only make the payment on an $82,000 loan. The purchaser in this case, by getting a favorable interest rate, has obtained an advantage equivalent to an $18,000 reduction in price. There is more than one way to get a bargain.

A similar situation occurred when I was selling real estate while attending college. An old brick commercial building was for sale at $35,000. My broker informed me that he could have sold it to the tenant, but the price was just too high. A widow who owned it had been told by her husband before his death that she shouldn't sell for less than $35,000. She lived above the commercial store and wanted to leave the area to live with her daughter in Arizona, but she wanted the building sold before she left. I had an idea. I asked my broker if I could try to sell the building to the tenant. With my broker's permission I met with the tenant and asked him if he would buy the building for $30,000 with $5,000 down. The tenant, whose previous offer of $25,000 with $5,000 down had been rejected, said he would. I asked the tenant if he would be willing to pay 7¼ percent interest on the balance of $25,000 over a twenty-year amortization if I could get the offer accepted. The tenant indicated that he would go along with that, but that the owner was stubborn and had that unrealistic $35,000 price in her head and I wouldn't be able to shake her.

I took out an amortization table and showed the tenant that the payments on a twenty-year, $25,000 loan at 7¼ percent came to $197.60 in principal and interest payments. I asked if those payments were satisfactory and the tenant said yes. I then told the tenant I thought he could buy the property with payments of $197.60 per month for twenty years. I looked up payments on $30,000 for twenty years at 5 percent interest. The payments amounted to $197.10 per month. I explained to the tenant that a $35,000 offer at 5 percent interest financing $30,000 resulted in virtually the same payment as financing $25,000 at 7¼ percent. I explained to the tenant that while a purchase under these terms would not give him as much interest to deduct, he would have greater depreciation since there would be $5,000 more in cost to depreciate.

My reasoning made sense to the tenant, and we made the offer of $35,000 with $5,000 down and a twenty-year amortization on the balance with interest of 5 percent. I explained to the owner that this offer resulted in higher payments than the $25,000 previous offer but that the interest rate was low. I explained to her how I got the buyer to make the offer. All she could see, however, was the $35,000 price, and she was signing the offer before I finished my explanation.

I have had other similar experiences. One case involved a corporation which was disposing of a fairly new warehouse they had built. I put in a reasonable but low offer which was countered with a full-price offer at a very low interest. The counter offer kept my payments the same as if they had accepted my original offer. The reason for this strange counter offer was that while they considered my offer reasonable, the corporate real estate officer did not want to sell the property below the book value. On paper, the sale at the higher price looked much better for the officer.

Actually, there is some disadvantage for the buyer in raising the price and cutting the interest. Since interest is a deductible expense while payment on the principal is not, you do lose tax deductions by this method. A seller should check with a CPA before accepting a below-market interest rate. The IRS may impute a higher interest rate and tax the seller as if it had been received, if the rate set is too low.

In the early 1960s I purchased a home in a new subdivision in Utah. The developer had a number of homes that were unsold. He turned down my original offer of $2,000 below his listed price. He told me that he had lived in the area all his life and if he gave me a bargain, other purchasers in the development would be unhappy. He said that someone at the savings and loan would talk about his cutting his prices and soon everyone would know.

I therefore presented a new offer for the full price contingent upon the seller agreeing to finish the basement and pour a patio slab at a price which was acceptable to me. I signed a separate agreement for this work at a price of $10. This really amounted to more than the $2,000 price reduction I had originally asked for, and the seller was pleased.

What I have learned is that while some element of a purchase may not be negotiable, there are usually negotiable aspects to any transaction.

VALUE AND PRICE ARE NOT ALWAYS THE SAME THING

Some people feel that if they cut a seller's asking price they have obtained a good deal. This is not necessarily the case. Be sure of the value before you make your offer, as the actual value may bear no relationship to the asking price.

I don't always try to cut price or terms. In a seller's market with many buyers and few sellers, I have learned not to try to save that last penny. If the listing price is right, make a full-price offer. While waiting for a counter offer, I lost a property I really wanted because another person submitted a full-price offer to the seller. I recently offered more than the listed price for a commercial building. There were two offers in on the property, one of which I believed to be a full-price offer. Since I wanted the property, I offered $10,000 over the listed price.

What you offer is your decision. If you wish to make an offer, don't worry that the real estate agent will say it won't be accepted; it is your offer. Keep in mind that the primary responsibility of the real estate agent is to get the best deal possible for the seller, not for you the buyer.

Again, don't ask your friends if you should buy a property. If they are not investing in real estate, they will probably tell you to play it safe as they are doing and not buy. People cannot very well tell others to invest while they themselves are timid about real estate investing.

A banker is a poor person to ask about a real estate investment. You can expect a negative reaction. Bankers are conservative and are generally not enthusiastic about real estate. They prefer nice, safe government bonds. If you are planning to withdraw funds from the bank to invest elsewhere, they will advise against it. They have a direct financial interest in your not buying real estate.

Look Before You Leap.   Don't rush to buy the deal that is too good to be true. Normally such a deal isn't true: there is usually something wrong. There are many sharp operators who are willing to lie, cheat and steal to get your money. A seller may "forget" to tell you that the property is in a flood plain and that a building permit will not be issued or that an addition was built without a permit and must be ripped down, as it violates building codes.

I was offered a commercial building at what appeared to be a bargain price. It was leased to a strong tenant, but the lease was about to expire. This didn't bother me, as the property could easily be rented if the tenant failed to sign a new lease. The owner had left the country to live in Europe and had listed it for sale with an agent. I checked with the tenant as to his intentions and was told that he had an option to purchase the property and had recently notified the owner of his intention to exercise the option. The option was for an appreciably lower price than the property was listed at. A purchase could have resulted in an expensive lawsuit as well as an actual loss.

BARGAINS MAY TURN UP

Several years ago I was offered a deal which also appeared too good to be true, a 12,000-square-foot building leased for ten years to a major national corporation. The price at which it was offered was far below the land and reproduction cost. The lease was a triple net lease whereby the tenant made all repairs and even paid the taxes and insurance. The net rent would be more than sufficient to make the payments. The seller was willing to carry the paper with a fairly low downpayment and a rate of interest well below the current market rate. The owner, however, was a sophisticated real estate attorney and this bothered me. Why was he offering such a good deal?

I checked with the local building inspector and the fire marshall for possible building violations. I also checked the city planning commission to find out what was happening in the area and to verify the zoning. I even met with the broker and the seller for lunch before I gave my offer. I ended up buying the property for $130,000 and $25,000 down. Incidentally, I appraised the land alone as being worth $100,000. Besides giving me an immediate positive cash flow, the property also provided me with the excellent tax benefit of depreciation. It is less than three years since I purchased the building. I turned down a $350,000 offer, as I feel it is worth more than that. This means that my $25,000 investment has given me an equity of at least $245,000. For the first time in my life I found a deal which looked too good to be true but was true. I still don't understand the seller's motivation.

VERIFY ALL FIGURES

Some brokers will give you pro forma statements on a property. These are estimates of future income and expenses. Don't take these estimates too literally. Generally, the expense estimates are unrealistically low and the income estimates unrealistically high.

Some owners will make deceptive rental claims. For instance, an owner might rent a unit for $300 per month when the market would justify only $250 per month. The owner might have given the tenant several months' free rent to sign a one-year lease. If this were the case, the tenant can be expected to leave at the end of the lease. The best way to verify rents is to talk with the tenants. You may find that things are not always as indicated in the leases.

I know of a case in which a buyer purchased a newly furnished apartment building. The rents appeared to be above what the market would indicate, but the buyer felt that this was because it was the only new building in the area. The buyer discovered that each of the tenants had rented during a promotion whereby they were given a document which gave them the right to buy the furniture in the apartment for only $100 if they stayed for eighteen months. What the new owner had in a few months was a number of vacant unfurnished units and a lawsuit against a former owner who "forgot" to mention the options.

When I request rental figures or operational costs from an agent or owner, I always ask that the figures be verified in writing. I very often find the attractive verbal figures are not the same as those put down in writing.

FRAUDULENT OFFERS

Free Lot Schemes. A con game you should watch out for is a free lot scheme. Often at fairs people are asked to fill out a card for a free drawing. What happens in a free lot scheme is that every adult who entered the drawing is notified that he or she is a winner of one of the grand prizes, a lot in a particular subdivision. Each winner is given the legal description of the lot and is told that he or she has a period of time, usually thirty days, to pay the itemized transfer fees, which will vary from $200 to $600, after which the winner will receive title to the lot.

Those who pay get a deed, but the lots used in these schemes are close to worthless. A fair lot value might be $50 to $100. What the free lot scheme has done is to allow a seller to get far more than the land can be sold for by giving it away. The buyers feel they are getting something for nothing and are quickly parted from their money. While the scheme is generally illegal, variations on it are constantly cropping up. Remember that the free lunch went out with the nickel beer.

Dinner Party Land Sales. The way these work is that you win, or are given, a free vacation with the condition that you attend a dinner party. You may be offered free Las Vegas show tickets for attending. One operator I know of would mail out a pair of tickets marked $50 each. With the tickets was a handwritten note addressed to the recipient, such as: "Jim, I can't use these tickets and I thought you would be interested. Please go as my guest. If you can't make it, see that the tickets are not wasted. M——" The signature on the note is illegible. Something for nothing does bring people in, so there is normally a full house.

Typically, guests will be taken to a table so as not to mix with other "marks." At the table will be a couple who are "shills" and a representative of the organization putting on the seminar. Cocktails are given freely. The waitresses make sure the guests know that everything is included with their ticket. The dinner is first class and usually includes wine. Brandy and cigars are then brought around.

A speaker will make an excellent presentation on the area to be sold with colored slides, movies and charts showing why the property offers unique opportunities for great profit. One typical story is that the parcels must be sold off so taxes can be paid; otherwise the owners would never sell with the land so close to development. I know one firm that uses older, very dignified actors to make the presentation.

A chart is usually put up showing available properties. It is usually indicated that when these few parcels are sold there will be no more available. This creates a sense of urgency. At each table the representative of the company will tout three or four parcels which he or she feels are superior deals. The representative will usually claim either that they are under-priced or that they are possible commercial property. The salespeople may also indicate that they have purchased a parcel themselves very near the parcels touted. The shill couple, who have become great friends with the mark couple, will show a great deal of interest and will buy a parcel. Usually these parcels require very low downpayments and are offered at attractive terms. The only problem is they may be overpriced by more than 1,000 percent.

The representative will yell out, "Put a hold on parcel number . . .!" Other salespeople are also yelling. People are carrying messages around as the board bristles with sold stickers. Activity seems frantic; there is an auction-like fever. Other parcels which the agent has touted will be reserved, leaving just one unsold.

The shill couple will try to talk their new friends into buying. Even people who are normally very conservative are apt to get caught up in the excitement and the lure of great profit. Usually the salesperson is successful. The shills and sales representative may split a 25 percent commission for the night's work on a lot selling from $4,000 to $6,000. There may be a legitimate dinner party land sales effort but if there is, I don't know of it. Always see property and verify its value before you buy.

Land Sale Thieves. Typically, land sale thieves buy land wholesale, break it up into lots or small acreage parcels and put it on the market at prices which bear no relationship to the market value. However, they do give excellent terms.

Several of these operators advertise for salespeople. They actually give these people intensive training, including real estate license training for which they charge a nominal fee. They really indoctrinate these potential salespeople in their project. Then the whole group of recruits are taken out to visit the site. The owner of the company tells them that they can't really expect to sell property unless they have faith in the property themselves. He offers each of them one lot or parcel, and one only, at 50 percent off the listed price. What happens is that a great number of salespeople buy lots. What the company was doing is grooming potential buyers, not potential salespeople.

Those who do go out and sell a few parcels are just a bonus for the land company.

> Many years ago on a Sunday drive I stopped to check out a land subdivision. The salespeople had four-wheel drive vehicles to take people out to see various parcels. The salesperson touted one particular 2½ acre parcel which he said I could get for $4,995 with only $495 down. (Don't be deceived; the price is $5,000 but $4,995 sounds much better.) The salesperson stopped at the office, ostensibly to pick up a map before he returned us to our car. He suggested we come in for a cold drink because it was a hot day and it might take him a while to find what he was after. The salesperson went into the next room and told another person we were interested in the particular $4,995 parcel. The other person explained there was a mistake, that it was a $6,500 parcel and it couldn't be sold for $4,995. My salesperson argued loudly on my behalf and the "boss" finally agreed to let him sell it for $4,995 because he had quoted this price, but there would be no commission for him on the sale. I imagine many people fell for this sudden bargain opportunity and this salesperson who fought so hard for them and didn't get paid.

I have lived in various desert communities for over fifteen years. Because desert land is cheap, it offers a great inventory for land sale schemes. Having written a number of real estate books, I am often contacted by people who want to know what their land is now worth. I refer these people to brokers and will no longer give any estimates of value. I have had several people get mad at me for telling them the truth. I was called a liar and physically threatened by one owner. Telling people that their $10,000 parcel on which they still owe $6,000 is worth only $2,000 is bound to upset them.

AUCTION SALES

This is a good way to buy property, but don't go to an auction unprepared. Know the property and set your top price and stick to it. It is easy to get caught up in the emotion of an auction setting. While an auction can provide a bargain, there are times when property at an auction will sell for far more than the market would otherwise indicate. Unless the seller has arranged financing, you should have your financing lined up in advance. An auction setting does not allow you to condition your offer. You as the offeror are usually making an unconditional offer to purchase at a stated price. The offer is not accepted by the auctioneer until the gavel falls.

WHEN YOU MAKE YOUR OFFER

If a property was put on the market very recently, it can sometimes be difficult to purchase it even though you are willing to meet the seller's price and terms.

The owner often gets the "greeds" when a full-price offer comes in right away. The owner feels he or she did not ask enough for the property and instead of accepting the offer the owner may either take the property off the market or raise the ante for the property.

Unless you believe that there is a great deal of competition for a property, it would probably be best not to make a full-price offer for a property listed only a day or two previously. A better approach would be an offer for less than the listed price and allowing only one day for acceptance. In this way you pressure the seller, who will either accept or come up with a counter offer. By accepting the counter offer, you will form a binding contract.

Using an Attorney.   Before you sign an offer, be sure you fully understand it. If it is not clear to you, see an attorney. This not only protects you, it also gives you peace of mind. There is a danger in accepting definitions from a real estate agent. The agent is giving you his or her opinion, which may not be the opinion a court would have should a disagreement arise. Always keep in mind that the first duty of the agent is to the owner, not you. The agent wants to make a commission. While most real estate agents are honest, there are some bad apples.

I recommend that you use an attorney to help you make your offers. You can ask an attorney in advance what the fees will be. Legal fees to prepare an offer are very small when compared with the obligations you are accepting with a purchase. You will want to develop a good relationship with an attorney specializing in real estate. In many states, attorneys with special training or experience are allowed to hold themselves out as real estate specialists.

I know several investors who customarily take their attorneys in with them as partners on their deals. They find the properties and their attorneys prepare offers and handle all legal matters. The two complement each other very well.

Consider All Financial Obligations.   Before you complete an offer, you should carefully consider the financial obligations. Can you make the payments? Don't count on a quick resale for a profit. By using amortization tables, which all real estate agents should have, you can compute your principal and interest payments. To this you should add an estimated amount for taxes, insurance and maintenance, as applicable. If you would like your own amortization tables, contact a title insurance company. Many give them away free.

QUICK AND CAREFUL ACTION

When a decision to buy is made, you should act quickly.

A broker called me on a new commercial listing he had in an area where I own property. I made an appointment to see the building the next day. The broker was busy so the tenant showed me the property. I was unable to get with the broker until the day after I saw the building. I submitted an offer with only a few minor changes from the price and terms requested in the listing. I was afraid a full-price offer might scare the seller. My offer was delivered to the owner just one hour after she had received and accepted another offer.

CONTINGENCY CLAUSES

If you really want a property, get your offer in without delay. If you are worried about something and want to check it out, you can make your offer *contingent upon* that item.

You can frequently tie up a property for a few days by placing a contingency on it:
Contingent upon the approval of _____ within _____ days of acceptance.

The approval person could be your spouse, a professional real estate counselor, a construction expert or any other appropriate person.

If you are unsure of your ability to finance a purchase, the following statement in an offer protects you from being in default should financing not be available:
Contingent upon obtaining an 80 percent loan at no more than 13 percent interest by [date].

If you want a zoning change, you could include:
Contingent upon a zoning change by [date], allowing fourteen apartments to be built on the site.

This sort of contingency can be dangerous as it may give the seller ideas which could result in a higher price.

If the property does not have a sewer, you want to make certain that a septic system is possible. You could state:
Contingent upon passing percolation test by [date].

If a property has a problem tenant or if you wish property for your own use, you can save cost, time and emotional drain by having the present owner remove the tenant. You might state:
Contingent upon owner delivering premises in a vacant condition at time of closing.

If your old property is highly saleable and the property you are purchasing has been on the market for some time, the seller may agree to the following contingency:

This offer is contingent upon the sale of the property at [address] by [date].

The following contingency is preprinted in many offers. It protects the buyer against easements or other problems that the buyer is unaware of.
Contingent on buyer's approval of preliminary title report.

Often, what a seller indicates a lease provides is not in fact what the lease states. You might consider:
Subject to seeing and approving existing leases.

If you have not checked local codes and have doubts as to a building's compliance with the codes, you certainly would want the following provision in your offer:
Subject to seller warranting that the building complies with all building, health and fire codes.

In an older building where you were only able to see one or two units, what you saw might possibly be the exceptional units, not representative of all the units. You might therefore wish the following contingency:
Subject to the inspection and approval of all units in the building by the buyer.

Don't take it for granted that a loan can be assumed. You should subject your offer to a loan assumption if the assumption is important to you. A clause such as the following is very common:
Subject to the assumption of a loan in the amount of approximately $____ at ____ percent interest with payments of $____ per month.

When an offer requires seller financing, you want the material terms of the financing spelled out in detail. For example:
Subject to the seller's taking back as part of the purchase price a second mortgage in the amount of $____ and payable at $____ or more per month. Said payment to include interest at ____ percent. This mortgage shall be due and payable in full in ____ years.

You will want the "or more" to be included since it will allow prepayment without any penalty. Most sellers will not accept a long-term second mortgage. Normally sellers want the buyers to agree to pay them off in five to seven years. Usually, because of appreciation, increased equity will allow refinancing to pay off this second mortgage.

If you have any doubts at all as to the income and expenses quoted, consider the following:
Subject to the seller warranting that the attached income and expense statement is accurate and complete for the period indicated.

If the statement provided was intentionally prepared falsely, the seller will probably refuse to accept this warranty.

To protect against a seller's failing to make repairs if items are broken or become inoperative prior to the closing, you might consider the following: *Subject to all electrical, plumbing and mechanical equipment being in good and proper working order as of [date].*

As a buyer you will want your offer to include a clause requiring the seller to maintain the garden, pool, buildings and other improvements until closing. Otherwise neglect could result in substantial damage.

You can tailor your contingencies to the special circumstances of a purchase. It is not wise, however, to include contingencies when they are not really needed. The more contingencies your offer contains, the less chance you have of getting acceptance. Use contingencies only when they are really important.

ASSUMING ASSESSMENTS

As a buyer you want your offer to read, "Seller to pay all special assessments." This means that bonded indebtedness for sewer, street, water and other services will be paid by the seller. This can really amount to the same thing as a reduction in price of several thousand dollars. Depending on the situation, you might consider a full-price offer but require the assessments be paid by the seller.

If you were a seller, you would want these assessments to be assumed by the buyer, which means that the buyer must pay them off as they become due.

INCOME PROPERTY

An offer for income property should require the seller to turn over all tenant deposits (security, key and last months' rent) at close of escrow. The money you get back could significantly reduce your cash requirements for closing the transaction. Of course all rents should be prorated at close of escrow.

ASSUMING LOANS

Even if you can pay cash or intend to refinance, if there are advantageous private loans on the property, you should try to assume them. After the purchase you can then contact the individuals holding the loans and offer to pay off the loans at a discount. You can usually negotiate some sort of discount for early payment. If the individual needs money, then the discount can be substantial.

I once obtained a 50 percent discount on a second mortgage. This discount actually amounted to more than a $5,000 price reduction after the purchase.

If the sellers will carry paper, let them, even if you could obtain similar conventional financing. Conventional lenders are not interested in discounting the loan for an early payment, but private individuals frequently are. After about six months, an offer of prepayment at a discount can be made. The seller might not accept at first, but it will be in the back of the seller's mind as a source of cash. There is an excellent chance that eventually the seller will make you a discount offer for prepayment.

Some loans cannot be assumed because of alienation clauses (also called due-on-sale clauses). These clauses say that if the property is alienated (conveyed), then the entire balance due on the loan is due in full. Several state courts have declared these clauses are not valid for loans by state-licensed lenders. In other states they are considered valid. You should check with your attorney as to the assumability of a specific loan. FHA and VA loans are assumable.

Many state courts hold that a land contract is not really a sale since the seller retains title until the contract is paid off. Therefore, you can take advantage of a below-market interest rate on an existing loan by offering to buy on a land contract.

If you are trying to get around an alienation clause or are considering buying on a land contract, have a real estate attorney advise you and prepare the offer.

ABSTRACTS AND TITLE INSURANCE

In many areas of the country, abstracts are used to verify title. An abstract is simply a copy of every recorded document dealing with the property. An attorney will read the abstract and give you an opinion as to the marketability of the title. Even though you use an attorney, there can still be problems with an abstract. An attorney would not know if a prior deed was forged or if a prior grantor had been declared insane or was otherwise incompetent prior to a conveyance. I therefore recommend that your offer specify that title shall be verified by a standard policy of title insurance paid for by the seller. Sellers often prefer abstracts since bringing an abstract up to date is usually less expensive than title insurance. The attorney who helps you might not particularly like this request, since title insurance has been making inroads into an area formerly held by lawyers alone. Title insurance means no abstract reading fees for the attorney.

You should consider purchasing an extended coverage policy of title insurance. As the buyer, you will be expected to pay this additional cost. An extended coverage policy provides additional protection for items such as incorrect survey or building on the wrong lot. Your title insurance company will explain the advantages of obtaining this additional coverage.

BALLOON PAYMENTS, REFINANCING AND FORECLOSURE

As a buyer you should be aware of the fact that if a loan has a balloon payment it means that the entire loan balance must be paid in one lump sum when due. If you are unable to obtain refinancing or otherwise cannot make the balloon payment, you could be foreclosed. Usually you can expect to obtain refinancing because of your increased equity. It is not wise to wait until the balloon payment is due to start looking for new financing. Have it arranged well in advance. Often, by agreeing to increase the interest rate before the balloon payment is due, you can persuade the person holding the loan to extend it.

If there is an existing, assumable loan, it might be better for you as a buyer to take subject to the loan rather than assume and agree to pay. When you take subject to a loan you don't really agree to be obligated to pay it. Of course, if you don't pay, you will be foreclosed and lose the property. But should you be foreclosed, no deficiency judgment is possible against you. If you assume a loan, you have agreed to be primarily liable on the loan, so default and foreclosure could possibly result in a deficiency judgment.

In some states deficiency judgments will not be granted and in other states they are difficult to obtain. Basically, a deficiency occurs when the foreclosure sale does not bring enough money to pay off the loan. In states allowing a deficiency judgment, the lender would demand to be reimbursed for the deficiency. It should be pointed out that foreclosures are rare and deficiency judgments are very rare, even where possible.

IS PERSONAL PROPERTY INCLUDED IN THE SALE?

Your offer should specify what personal property is included in the sale. By spelling things out you can avoid misunderstandings later. For example, if there is a swimming pool, does the pool cleaning equipment stay? Does a portable metal storage building stay? What about the drapes, slide-in ranges, fireplace screens and tools? Be specific. You can frequently induce sellers to include personal property such as washers, dryers and refrigerators, which they did not intend to include, by asking for them in the offer. This really serves as the equivalent of an additional cut in price.

Because personal property located in income property can be depreciated in a much shorter period of time than real property, you might want to specify in an offer for furnished units how much of the offer applies to the real property and how much applies to the personal property. Chances are you will want to allocate the maximum amount possible to the personal property. A CPA can help you in making decisions in this area.

SELLER OR BUYER RESPONSIBILITY?

If an owner is selling property "as is," you should be particularly careful. Look for the unexpected. Just because you buy a property "as is" does not, however, mean that you have given up all your rights. If a seller knows of a hidden defect and fails to inform the buyer or actually conceals the defect, many courts will hold the seller liable despite the fact that the purchase was "as is."

If the seller is not giving up possession until after closing, your offer should cover the rent, if any, which the seller is to pay. The offer should also cover who is to be responsible for a casualty loss to the property, such as fire, prior to possession.

RENT ARREARAGES

For income properties, rent arrearages should be agreed upon. As a buyer you don't want to pay the seller for these arrearages as they may not ever be collected from the tenants. It can be a bookkeeping headache to try to collect them for the seller and then remit them. As a buyer I just ask that all claims for past-due rentals be assigned to me as part of the consideration for the purchase price. If they are collectible, it is something extra; if not, I am not out.

TAKING TITLE

Most offers to purchase will state the manner of taking title. One way to cover this is to write that "title shall vest in _____ or assignee as directed by purchaser during escrow." By including "assignee" you can have a double escrow. This means that if you sell the property prior to the real estate closing, you can provide that the title will go directly to your purchaser from the seller. You can thereby avoid closing costs, since your purchaser will pay them.

LIQUIDATED DAMAGES

Unless agreed otherwise, a purchaser who defaults can be held liable for damages by the seller. If the seller later completes a sale at a lower price, then the difference would be the seller's damages. I believe it is best to include a liquidated damages provision. Liquidated damages are damages agreed to in advance of any breach of contract, to be paid should the buyer default. Customarily in real estate transactions, the agreement is that the buyer forfeit the earnest money deposit as the damages. This is then the sole remedy which the seller can have against the buyer. As a buyer you might not want to forfeit the deposit if it were substantial, but you would probably want the liquidated damages agreement if the downpayment is low.

CONFIRMING A SERIOUS OFFER

I normally give a substantial earnest money check with my offers. It indicates that I am a serious buyer. A large earnest money check makes it harder for a seller to refuse an offer. I provide in my offers that the earnest money check is not to be cashed until my offer is accepted. This means that I do not actually have to commit dollars until I know I have a deal. In this manner I can leave money in interest-bearing accounts until it is actually required.

RELEASE CLAUSES AND BLANKET ENCUMBRANCES

If you are purchasing several parcels from one seller or a parcel which can conceivably be broken into several parcels, your offer should contain a release clause from any blanket encumbrance. A blanket encumbrance is a lien covering more than one property, such as a single mortgage over several properties. The release clause provides for the release of separate parcels from the lien upon payment of stated amounts. Without the release clause, you could not resell one parcel without paying off the entire blanket loan.

ACCEPTANCE OF OFFERS

Your offer to purchase should state how long it is good for. If no period is specified, the offer is considered to be open for a reasonable period of time. Even though you may allow a number of days for acceptance of your offer, you have the right to withdraw your offer any time prior to acceptance.

Acceptance is generally considered to take place upon the mailing of the seller's written acceptance. Once the seller has placed the acceptance in the mail, you can no longer revoke your offer. Revocation, on the other hand, takes place upon receipt. Therefore, even though you have mailed your revocation of your offer, it can be accepted by the seller up to the time your revocation is actually received.

I do not believe in giving the seller very much time to accept an offer. If the seller is in the community, I only provide one day for acceptance. This forces a decision and usually avoids a situation where the seller runs around and gets the advice of numerous people. The seller's friends are likely to tell him or her what he or she wants to hear, which is "Why, your property is worth lots more than that!" Often unexpert advice causes sellers to lose advantageous sales.

You should not let real estate agents dictate your offer; the offer is yours, not theirs. While you want expert advice, especially from attorneys and accountants, remember that you are the one who is agreeing to pay.

No man acquires property without acquiring with it a little arithmetic also.

—Ralph Waldo Emerson, 1850

10

Subdividing—Smaller Can Be Better

Whoever first said that the whole is equal to the sum of its parts didn't have the slightest idea what subdividing is all about. In real estate the value of a large parcel can be considerably less than the value of the property when cut up into smaller, more usable units. For example, a twenty-acre parcel might have a market value of $3,500 per acre, or $70,000. If the twenty-acre parcel were broken into four parcels of five acres each, they might sell for $25,000 each, or $100,000 total. If the parcel were broken into one-acre parcels, they might well sell for $8,000 each, or $160,000 total. As parcels are cut into smaller acreage pieces, there is an increased demand since more buyers can afford to buy and use the smaller parcels.

Today we have many different types of subdivisions—recreational, conventional housing, mobile home and even industrial properties.

LAKE DEVELOPMENT

If land has a creek or spring and proper topography, there is the possibility of developing a lake. Lake developments, whether natural or manmade, offer exceptional investment opportunity for future residential development. Water-related property sells at a great premium. Some developers simply locate property and put in the lakes, after which they wholesale the parcel to a developer for final development.

A close friend recently paid $15,000 down on a $150,000 purchase price for a 160-acre parcel containing a 40-acre lake. He spent $9,000 for engineering work and $28,000 for some land clearing and bulldozing of roads. An additional $11,000 was spent improving a beach and park area. My friend has recently started selling the parcels. He has forty-five lake lots of 100 feet or more which he is selling at an average price of $10,000. The rest of the lake frontage is owned in

95

common by the back lot owners who have the improved beach and park area. A permanent dock and boat landing is on the common area. There are only twenty-five back lots, from two to five acres in size. The average price of the back lots is also $10,000. My friend hopes to gross $700,000 on the project and have a net profit of over $450,000, on a total cash investment of $63,000. So far he has sold eighteen parcels in the first three months, so it looks as if his projections are realistic. He is selling the parcels with low downpayments and is carrying the paper at 10 percent interest. When his collected interest is added to his profit, he should take out over $1,000,000 in profit from this single development.

RECREATIONAL SUBDIVISIONS

Recreational subdivisions are usually located within one tank of gas from a major metropolitan area. The subdivider often builds a club house and sometimes other facilities such as a central stable. The acreage parcels usually have water to them as well as electricity. Buyers can use them for camping or build cabins on them. Many of these developments include a shell or unfinished cabin at a reasonable price.

There have been a number of unusual recreational clubs which are similar to subdivisions. I know of one which has a club house and 1,000 camping or trailer sites. Buyers don't get their own site, just the right to use an available site. The club has sold 4,000 life memberships. While there are more members than sites, it is unlikely that all of the sites will be occupied at one time.

OWN-YOUR-OWN-LOT MOBILE HOME PARKS

The lots are small, usually about fifty by seventy-five feet. Even with the loss of land for streets and public areas, developers may still obtain from six to ten lots per acre. In many cases these lots sell for upwards of $20,000. The attraction these subdivisions have is that many mobile home buyers have heard about lot owners raising the rents very high after the park is filled. Today mobile homes are not really mobile at all, as moving can be impractical. Coach owners therefore often feel that they are at the mercy of the park owners. They would rather make a higher payment and know that they are buying their own lot and protecting themselves against rent increases.

Some park owners have turned existing parks into condominiums. It is a way to sell the park quickly and obtain a premium price. Because of the immobile nature of today's installed mobile homes, the buyers are right there; they are the current renters. Everyone benefits in this type of sale. The park owner gets a premium price and the lot buyers, while possibly paying more each month toward rent, can now deduct the interest from their taxes. The net effect for many of the buyers will be a lower true monthly cost.

OLDER LAKE RESORTS

These are generally poor investments for operators, who will often sell far below reproduction costs and with favorable terms. In recent years a number of investors have been actively buying these resorts and breaking them up. While a large resort operating at a loss might not be desirable, individual vacation cabins appeal to a large market.

THE SUBDIVISION PROCESS

While the subdivision process sounds simple, it can actually be quite involved. There are local, state and even federal regulations concerning subdivisions. Large subdivisions also require environmental impact reports, which can be costly. The average time for subdivision approval varies by state and community. In some areas it takes only a few months, while in other areas, such as Los Angeles, a three-year period to obtain all approvals is not unusual.

Although the raw land can usually be purchased with little money down, the payments must be made on the land; therefore, a developer must have sufficient cash flow to make the payments during approval and development stages.

Residential subdivisions in some areas must be fully improved. This can mean sewer, water, streets, curb, gutter and even sidewalks. This type of subdivision can require expenditures of thousands of dollars for every lot. Because of the development costs, many subdividers develop in phases, such as 50 lots at a time in a development which will contain perhaps 500 lots total.

While large subdivisions can require a great deal of time and effort, a simple split of a parcel into two parcels can usually be accomplished with little difficulty. In most states you can manufacture as many as four parcels from a single parcel with relatively few problems. Your local building department or planning commission can tell you what state and local procedures and regulations govern the subdivision process.

RELEASE CLAUSES

When you purchase property which you are considering splitting, you should provide in your mortgage or trust deed a release clause or a provision for separate liens on the parcels. A release clause allows you to sell one parcel free and clear of the mortgage upon the payment of a specified sum of money. Without a release clause or a provision for separate liens, the only way you could sell one of the parcels would be by land contract. If someone wanted to pay cash, you could not give clear title unless you paid off the blanket lien covering all the parcels.

WHOLESALING PARCELS

The great cost in time and money of getting a subdivision approved opens up an entirely new field for investors with vision—wholesaling parcels with approvals for developers who want to build right now. The investor gets the proper zoning changes, has the engineering work completed and obtains all approvals. This work can be worth much more than its cost to a developer. Keep in mind that payments must be made on the land while this approval work is taking place. Also, what is finally approved can often turn out to be much less desirable than what was originally contemplated. For instance, the density approved might be much less than what was originally requested.

There are people who will handle the detail work of a subdivision approval for you at a fee, but if you intend to handle more than one subdivision, you should get involved in the detail work so you fully understand what is required.

Before getting involved in any subdivision project, you should consider all the costs as well as the time required. As a rule of thumb, you should carefully estimate the time required from land acquisition to the first sale, and then double this time. After carefully estimating all development costs, you should add 50 percent to the figure. If the project does not look economically feasible based on these estimations, I would not recommend it. It is seldom that initial time and cost estimates come close to the actual costs. Don't count on being lucky. Because of the many uncertainties involved in subdivision approval and land preparation, you should leave a sufficient profit margin to cover the worst contingencies. Many years ago I all but lost my shirt when I leveraged myself into a large project which had serious delays. I found myself unable to continue to bear the costs. Time delays can turn what looks like a sure profit into a loss.

INDUSTRIAL PARKS

Industrial parks offer exceptional profit potential. Generally they should be located close to good transportation arteries. A railroad siding is not required for many light manufacturing plants. However, large water mains and good water pressure are essential for sprinkler systems. Possible heavy electrical demands require the availability of three-phase wiring. Adequate sewage disposal is also required. In some better industrial parks in Orange County, California, lots are selling as high as ten dollars per square foot. This is almost one-half million dollars per acre.

CONDOMINIUM CONVERSIONS

Perhaps the greatest opportunities for small investors are in the condominium conversion area of subdivisions. In a conversion situation you are usually simply changing from rental units to units owned by the individual occupants. One of my colleagues who has done amazingly well at condominium conversions calls them the greatest idea since sliced bread.

A few years ago, in many areas, housing could not be purchased for under $50,000. At the same time, apartment buildings could be purchased at perhaps $25,000 per unit. A person who purchased a ten-unit, two-bedroom building for $250,000 could get the required approvals and convert the existing building into ten condominium units which could be sold for $50,000 each. If the buyer had purchased the building with $50,000 down, then the $250,000 profit would be a profit of 500 percent on the downpayment. This may seem like a huge profit, but there have been thousands of condominium conversions with profits of this magnitude. Because of the demand, as more people have realized the potential for conversions, apartment prices have soared. Nevertheless, substantial profits are still being made.

In some conversions, over half the units have been sold to the actual tenants. By buying their units, they don't have to move. While the tenants must make a monthly payment significantly higher than their previous rent, as buyers they can deduct interest and taxes as an expense for their federal and state income tax. In some cases these deductions can offset the difference in monthly expenses.

STOCK COOPERATIVES

In some states, a stock cooperative can avoid many of the approvals required for a condominium. A condominium is an actual subdivision with one property broken up into small units with individual owners. A stock cooperative is not truly a subdivision in that the cooperative corporation takes title to the entire building. Each stockholder has rights to occupy a unit but doesn't really own it. There is likely to be more buyer resistance to a cooperative than to a condominium. A cooperative has dangers connected with singular ownership. Since there is only one mortgage, if several owners fail to pay their share, the mortgage covering the entire building can be foreclosed.

CURRENT TREND TO CONDOMINIUM CONVERSION

Some investors specialize in buying an apartment, getting the condominium approvals and selling it. In some cases they can use options and get the approvals during the option period. The investors can sell the buildings readily with the conversion approvals. In this manner large profits are possible; the only investment is the price paid for the option.

We have been seeing the growth of community hostility toward condominium conversions of apartments. In some areas a moratorium has been placed on these conversions. Because lower-income and elderly people have often been forced to leave their homes after many years because a new buyer wants to make a profit, we can understand the resentment against condominium conversions. In the future, a great deal of local legislation is likely to restrict the right of an owner to convert apartment units to condominiums.

Today's business people are sophisticated in tax matters. They realize that ownership offers several tax advantages over renting. Besides the fact that interest and tax payments are deductible, ownership offers the further tax benefit of depreciation. Furthermore, the increase in commercial space rentals has made many realize the desirability of controlling their outlay for space requirements so as not to be at the mercy of an inflationary economy. In addition, ownership is an investment which can be expected to increase in value and, as such, is a hedge against inflation.

COMMERCIAL CONDOMINIUMS

In the late 1960s and early 1970s some commercial condominiums had difficulty selling out. I don't believe that this will be the situation now. These earlier condominiums came at a time when the condominium concept was not widely accepted. In addition, the economy was relatively stable and major rent increases were not a serious threat to business. The time may now be ripe for commercial condominiums.

Condominium conversions of shopping centers and even the building of new shopping centers as condominiums offer exceptionally good profit potential. Such conversions can appeal to strong local tenants. They offer the merchant guaranteed, long-term space costs and the tax advantage of depreciation, as well as appreciation possibilities. Intelligent commercial tenants should be readily willing to pay one-fourth to one-third more in monthly purchase costs than they would for rent payments.

There is a large medical office building located next to a hospital. The building is one story and has seventeen suites of offices. Several of the doctors used to own the building. Because of the death of one owner and the break-up of an association between two other doctors, the building was for sale. A former evening student of mine purchased the building for $500,000. He gave the owners $50,000 cash, assumed a $300,000 loan and agreed to pay the $150,000 balance within three years. The price appeared very low for the building, but the rents were quite low and the owners paid the utilities. All the offices were on one-year leases which expired at various times.

My former student first removed the central air-conditioning units and put in separate roof units for each suite of offices, costing him approximately $60,000. After getting subdivision approval, he offered the units to the individual doctors. He sold fourteen units to the occupants, and three of the buyers also purchased adjacent units which the occupants did not wish to purchase. This student sold the units at prices ranging from $58,000 to $87,000, with an average price of $76,000 or a gross sales price of $1,292,000. All the units were sold with a 20 percent downpayment, or $258,000 down. He therefore had enough money to pay off the sellers' equity of $150,000, and almost completely reimbursed the buyer for all the cash expended. He then owed only $300,000 on the project and had $1,034,000 due him, or an equity of over $700,000. Since the $300,000 mortgage was at 8 percent and the doctors were paying 10 percent interest on their units, he also makes a 2 percent interest differential on the $300,000, plus the interest on his equity. Over the next twenty years the student will be taking over $2,000,000 out of this property in which is now left only $2,000 of his own money.

I would like to take credit for this project, but I can't. My former student put it together entirely by himself. He had analyzed the situation well. The points he considered were:

1. This was the only truly first-class office facility in a city of about 30,000 people.
2. It was next to the hospital and there was no vacant land in the hospital area.
3. The doctors were all on one-year leases, so they would not have too much time to locate or build other space.
4. The money market at the time was extremely tight in the area, so that it would have been difficult and expensive to build any new medical facility.
5. While his purchase price was low, construction costs were high. His sales prices were not out of line with construction costs.
6. He was offering as an added inducement an interest rate at least 4 percent below the current money market for loans on commercial property.

CONDOTELS

Some motels have begun converting to condominiums. They call themselves condotels. The management will rent the unit when the owner is not there as a regular motel unit, and the owner shares the gross receipts with the management. These units have been primarily in resort areas. I don't expect this concept to be highly successful for several years yet.

TIME SHARES

One concept whose time appears to have arrived is the time share. The owners normally buy the use of a resort area condominium unit for one week or more per year. The buyer is thus assured of a place to vacation at a guaranteed cost. Typically, the time-share management will buy a block of units in a project developed by others. The management sets prices on the units so that the gross profit is at least 200 percent. For example, if a unit is purchased for $100,000, the management will try to sell fifty weeks at prices which average $6,000 each. Naturally, some weeks are more desirable and will sell for more than the average, while undesirable periods will sell for far less than the average. Usually the operators leave one or two weeks free for general refurbishing of the units. The owners of a week can use it, or the management will rent it for them. Some operators have time-share units in many locations and also handle vacation trades. While the markup of the units may sound high, you should consider that the time-share developers must make the payments until the units are sold, that some weeks are very undesirable and may take a long time to sell and that these sales involve heavy promotional and sales expenses including fifty sales commissions for each unit.

While time sharing is a fairly new concept, there is already some strong opposition. Hotels and resorts oppose time sharing since these units are directly competing with them for the same clientele. Some communities with hotel room tax are afraid that time-share units in the area will reduce hotel room occupancy and reduce their tax revenue. Other owners of units in developments having time-share units object to the intensive use of the common areas these units cause. Some time-share units have turned quiet residential condominium communities into noisy resorts.

UNDERSTANDING CONDOMINIUM CONVERSIONS

If you are interested in any type of condominium conversion, I recommend you contact your state real estate department, which normally handles state approvals. You should fully understand the procedures required for conversion. You might find that there are different requirements for apartments and condominiums. In some cases additional expenses such as garages may be required, or the local requirements may totally preclude an economical conversion. If you are uncertain as to whether or not approval for conversion will be granted, try to tie the property up with an option while you seek approval.

You should fully analyze the market for the converted units. Consider whether or not they will be saleable to the present tenants. Consider what the individual units will sell for. Then, if the profit potential justifies the risks, go ahead.

For any condominium or condominium conversion you should consider covenants, conditions and restrictions (CC&Rs). An attorney specializing in real estate can help you in this area. CC&Rs which meet the needs of other condominium projects might not be applicable to your project. CC&Rs are rules binding on each owner concerning, for example, the use of the premises and the number and type of pets allowed.

BUYING AND RESELLING

It is possible to make money buying units in a condominium or subdivision and holding them for resale. When lots in subdivision and condominium units appear to be selling out, it can be a good time to buy. If the lots or units are desirable, the prices generally show a significant increase after the last sale at the developer's prices.

In the first phase of a large development, when demand appears exceptionally strong, it can be wise to purchase before the first phase is sold out. Normally, the developer will raise the prices on the future stages of development in order to maximize the profit.

In some states, units may be started prior to final subdivision approval. While the developer is allowed to take a deposit as a reservation on a unit, the actual sale cannot be consummated until the subdivision has final approval. These deposits are customarily refundable. If the subdivision is very desirable, all the units will be reserved. In this case, saleable reservations can become valuable. I know of $1,000 reservations selling for over $25,000. If the reservation is not transferable, you can go through with the purchase and then resell the unit. If the units are not selling, you can ask for the return of your deposit, and all you have lost is the interest on the deposit.

ASSEMBLAGE

The opposite of subdividing is assemblage, the process of assembling several small contiguous parcels to make one large parcel. In areas which have become fully developed, it is difficult to find any large parcels. While smaller parcels are usually relatively more valuable, large parcels can in some circumstances be worth far more than their separate parts.

In the early 1960s I obtained an option to buy an old, vacant commercial garage building. I paid $100 for the right to buy the building for $75,000. It was located on a large, deep corner lot 150 by 300 feet in an old section of the city. Because the neighborhood was near the central city, many old homes there had recently been torn down to be replaced by new apartment buildings. Since the building was located on a major street and there were no major markets in the area, I approached all the food chains about my location. One of the chains liked the location but stated that my lot was far too small. They told me that if I could obtain a minimum of three acres at that location they would pay $250,000. This agreement was put in writing for me. I needed the five homes adjacent to the garage to make up the three acres. The row of small frame houses were on lots 60 by 300 feet. The recent sale price of these homes had been from $9,000 to $12,000. Two of the homes were for sale, and I was able to get thirty-day options to buy them at $15,000 each, which was above the listing prices. One of the homes was owned by a broker. We verbally agreed to an option at $16,000, but when I presented the option in writing, he wanted $20,000, so I had one $20,000 option. One of the owners didn't like the idea of moving, so I found a nicer brick home a few blocks away and got an option to purchase it for $14,500. The owner of the house I wanted agreed to give me the option of trading the nicer home for his house. Unfortunately, I had trouble with the home two houses down from the garage. The gentleman who lived there did not want to sell. He was retired and had a pension from his former employer and social security. He had a beautiful garden including a grape arbor. While his wife liked the idea of selling, he had no intention of leaving. I offered him $25,000 for his property. The answer was still no. I found a new house on a huge lot and showed it to him, offering a trade. His answer was still no. In desperation I contacted the two sons of the homeowner and had a meeting. I laid my cards on the table. I showed them the agreement I had from the food chain and all my options. The sons told me they would get back to me. The next day we met again with their attorney present. They offered to get their father to sell, but I would pay their father $15,000 for his house plus one-half of my profit on the entire deal. I verbally agreed to this because a reduced profit is better than none. The attorney stated he would put our agreement in writing and we would meet the next day. When we met, the attorney told me had contacted the supermarket chain and told them he represented my "partners." He had indicated that the entire parcel of over three acres was locked up now but, because of unexpectedly high acquisition costs, we could not sell it for $250,000. The attorney got the supermarket chain to agree to a $350,000 price. I was angry that he went around me. I try to live up to my word and, while I may negotiate hard, I don't try to make a new deal once I have reached an agreement. Although I had not really understood the value of a large parcel in this area, I would not have put the squeeze on the supermarket like this. Nevertheless, we now stood to split $350,000 after our acquisition costs of $154,500. This profit of $195,500 would mean $97,750 for me.

I wish I could say everything went smoothly, but it didn't. The sons, who were sure their father would follow their advice, were mistaken. Even their attorney couldn't get the father to sell. In a way it was funny, because the two sons, smitten by greed, practically went berserk trying to get the old man to sell.

I did make a small profit because I sold my option to buy the garage and the house next to it to a developer, who eventually built an apartment building on the site.

In every deal there are many things that can go wrong. For every effort rewarded by profit, there are usually many that are unproductive. I have learned that those people who do well in any business concentrate on probabilities and not on possibilities.

No man but feels more of a man in the world if he has a bit of ground that he can call his own. However small it is on the surface, it is four thousand miles deep and that is a very handsome property.
—*Charles Dudley Warner, 1871*

11

Trading Up To Wealth

Exchanging goes back to earliest times. It is the oldest form of commerce. By giving up something desired less, it is possible to acquire something desired more. While some may regard barter as primitive, it has been rediscovered as an exciting new real estate technique useful in our society.

TAX ADVANTAGES

One reason for the modern interest in exchanging is the Internal Revenue Code. An outright sale can result in a taxable gain, but Section 1031 of the Internal Revenue Code allows a tax-free exchange between like-for-like properties. What this means is that property which has been held for investment, trade or business can be traded for other property held for investment, trade or business. Therefore, a tax-free exchange is possible even though the character of the property exchanged is not similar. For example, vacant land can be traded for an apartment building. Real property must be traded for real property and personal property must be traded for personal property to qualify as a tax-free exchange.

Since a personal residence is not held for investment, trade or business, it does not qualify for a tax-free exchange. It is possible to change the character of your residence so that it would qualify. If you move out and rent your residence, it becomes an investment property. Many exchange experts advise that a residence must be rented a minimum of one year to qualify for a 1031 exchange.

Generally, property of dealers will not qualify for tax-free exchanges since it was acquired or developed by the dealers for resale. It may be subject to regular income tax, even though it is traded rather than sold.

Recent spectacular increases in property value have increased the interest in exchanging. Exchanging allows an owner to avoid taxation. While tax evasion is illegal, tax avoidance is simply good business practice.

BOOT

Not all exchanges are tax free. If one person receives "boot," the boot is fully taxable. Boot is unlike property given to even out a trade. Although it is usually money, boot can be personal property such as an automobile or jewels. Assume you were to trade a property which you own free and clear worth $50,000 for a property also held free and clear worth $40,000. If the other party were to give you $10,000 in cash to even up the trade, this boot would be taxable. One way to avoid a tax liability would be to have the other party use the $10,000 to buy a second property, and then trade two properties for your one property.

If one party to an exchange gets debt relief, because the property traded had a greater indebtedness than the new property acquired, then the amount of debt relief is taxable as capital gains. As an example, assume I own a property on which I owe $5,000 and I trade it even for a property which is free and clear of debt. The trade has resulted in my being relieved of $5,000 of debt, which is treated as boot and is taxable.

A number of years ago I was asked to help a farmer who had purchased 3,000 acres of arid land in 1945. He had paid between five and fifteen dollars per acre. He had only a marginal operation dry farming the land. The farmer received an offer of $1,000 per acre, or $3,000,000 for the farm. The purchaser was a large land sales firm which intended to subdivide the land into small parcels and sell them to investors.

The farmer came to me for advice. At the time of this offer, for capital gains purposes 50 percent of gain was taxable (not the current 40 percent). We estimated the tax liability for the sale at close to $1,000,000. I asked the farmer what he wanted to do with the money. He said he was too young to retire and wanted to continue farming. Also, he had two sons who wanted to be farmers. When I asked where he would most like to farm, he said Oregon. I had him and his sons take a trip to Oregon where they found a large farm to their liking. It had apples, crops and cattle and could be purchased at under $3,000,000.

The deal we worked out was that the developer purchased the Oregon farm, built a large new home on the farm, made several other specified improvements and traded it for the 3,000 acres. The farmer did take $200,000 in cash for operational expenses. While this boot was taxable, the rest of the trade avoided taxation.

This is probably a typical case of an exchange to avoid taxation. It involves three parties: the farmer, the developer and the owner of the Oregon farm. Actually, two-party exchanges are relatively rare. It is seldom you can find two parties who each want what the other party has. Multiple-party exchanges of three or even more parties are fairly common.

OTHER ADVANTAGES IN EXCHANGING

Taxation isn't the only reason for an exchange. People exchange to solve problems. By exchange they are able to get rid of a set of circumstances which they are not happy with for a set of circumstances they desire. Exchange can solve a great number of problems.

Depreciation. One reason for exchange is to get depreciation or greater depreciation. A property which does not offer any depreciation, such as raw land, can be traded for improved property, such as an apartment building, which can be depreciated for tax purposes. A smaller property can also be traded up to a much more expensive property, which increases the depreciation possible.

  Exchange allows you to change the ratio of land to improvements, which can allow greater depreciation. As an example, suppose you own a property worth $100,000 which has a structure on it worth only $20,000. You would be limited to depreciation of the improvements since the land cannot be depreciated. If you were to trade for a property also worth $100,000 but with improvements worth $90,000, you could depreciate from 90 percent of your original cost base. Since depreciation is only a paper expense, it shelters other income from taxation.

Geography. Some people exchange for geographical reasons. Assume a person who owns an apartment building in New York wishes to retire to Florida. Trading for an apartment building in Florida would fulfill the need without the necessity of a sale.

Income Gain. Some people trade to gain income. For instance, raw land, a cash drain because of taxation and no income, can be traded for apartments or commercial property offering a spendable cash flow. On the other hand, some people are willing to trade income property for raw land since they are more interested in appreciation than income and raw land tends to have greater appreciation than income property.

Clearing Debts. Some investors become conservative and want to eliminate debt. As an example, prior to retirement a person might trade a large, heavily mortgaged apartment project for a much smaller, free and clear property.

Pyramiding Property. Many other investors use exchange to pyramid their property. Being a "bull" when it comes to real property investments, I recommend this method strongly, especially for young investors. Smaller properties, even when purchased with low downpayments, can in a few years result in a substantial equity. By trading up, you increase the value of the property you own as well as increasing your indebtedness. Assume you traded a property worth $200,000 on which you owe $100,000 for a property worth $600,000 with a $500,000 indebtedness. While your equity in the property is the same, you are in a much better position as to appreciation. An increase in value of 50 percent in five years with the $200,000 property would have increased your equity from $100,000 to $200,000. For the $600,000 property the same 50 percent increase in value would now give you a $400,000 equity.

Of course, trading up does lower your percentage equity in a property. There are risks associated with this practice. A high vacancy factor or unexpected expenses could result in a large negative cash flow.

Consolidation of Property. Exchanging also allows consolidation of property. A number of smaller properties can be exchanged for one large property which is easier to manage. On the other hand, some owners are interested in diversifying. By obtaining several properties they can reduce their risk. This is especially true in the case of a large property with only one or two tenants.

Fewer Managerial Problems. Some people exchange to divest themselves of management problems. An apartment house with many problems could be exchanged for raw land which requires no real management.

Saleability. A property not readily saleable might be exchanged for a more saleable property. In such a case the exchange is simply an intermediate step toward a desired conclusion.

Avoiding a Realized Loss. There are times when an owner exchanges in order to avoid realizing a loss. Just as there is no realized loss for a stock market investor until the stock is sold, an owner of real property does not suffer a loss until the real property is sold. Some people psychologically do not want to admit the loss. We see this in the stock market when stock owners hold stock which has gone down for many years, hoping it will increase in value enough so they can break even. Even though there are other stocks they would prefer, they still hold on. When the same thing happens in real estate, trading is a solution. A trade allows owners to get into circumstances they prefer without admitting the loss.

I wanted to purchase a lot owned by a corporation. The price quoted to me by a corporate officer was far in excess of the current market. The corporation had purchased the lot several years previously, after

it had been announced that a major shopping center was to be built in the area. The shopping center was never built and land prices, having risen on the speculation of great development, had fallen.

During a luncheon meeting I discovered the corporation did not want to show a significant loss by the sale. It was a fairly small corporation and the loss would upset some of the stockholders. They preferred to hold on to the lot until it was worth what they had paid. I recognized this as an ideal exchange opportunity. I was holding a number of second mortgages on property I had previously sold. These mortgages, if sold, would be worth far less than their face value. My offer was to trade several of these mortgages at face value for the lot. It was accepted. The corporation got their price, although over a period of years, and I got the lot. The trade met the needs of both parties. Since mortgages are regarded as personal property, this was not a like-for-like, tax-free exchange. However, in this case, taxes were not an important consideration since neither of us was really making a profit on the trade.

Most people can be made interested in exchanging once they understand it. People usually want cash in order to purchase something. If they can get that something else directly, then there is really no reason for a sale.

WHAT YOU CAN EXCHANGE

In exchanging, even junk land has value. Junk land is land which serves no real purpose other than to help hold the world together. When an owner simply desires to get out of a set of circumstances, even junk land will be considered. To make junk land more attractive in an exchange, some sweetener such as cash can be added.

You can trade just about anything. You can trade the land and keep the building as a lessee or even trade the building and keep the land as a lessor. In some states mineral rights are considered real property. You can trade all the mineral rights to a property or perhaps half the mineral rights. Whatever has value can be traded.

Personal property can readily be traded, but remember that personal property cannot be traded for real property on a tax-free exchange since the trade is not like-for-like. This problem comes up in trading furnished units. The furniture is considered taxable boot unless the property traded for includes furniture of the same value.

Some attorneys claim there is a way to have a tax-free exchange of real property for personal property. These attorneys feel that by placing the personal property in a corporate shell and the real property in another corporate shell, they can have a like-for-like exchange of corporate stock. I think this method will work, but I do not know if there have been any tax rulings on it.

If you own your house or other property, you can get into real estate exchanging without giving up your property by manufacturing paper. It is fairly easy to find a seller who will take a second mortgage on your property as the downpayment for another property. If an owner is willing to carry a great deal of paper on a sale, the seller is obviously not that interested in receiving the cash. The purpose of the downpayment is simply security. By taking a downpayment in the form of a second mortgage, not only does the seller retain a security interest in the property sold, but also has a security interest in your property because of the paper given as a downpayment.

As values increase, it is possible to create more paper and use your increasing equity as downpayments on other property without selling your property. Of course you must realize that when you create a second mortgage you are obligating yourself to a payment.

PROBLEMS TO WATCH FOR

Unfortunately, there are many sharpies operating in exchange; these operators hope to give something of very low value for something of great value. They are not looking for an exchange partner; they are looking for a sucker. Don't take the word of another as to what a property is worth. It is only good business to check out comparable values in the area. If in doubt, you should seek the aid of a professional appraiser.

If taxes are a consideration in a trade, you should seek the advice of an attorney or a CPA who is knowledgeable in exchanges. Because of the specialized nature of exchanging, only a few attorneys and CPAs are really knowledgeable in this area. Most attorneys and CPAs will refer you to a competent specialist.

DELAYED EXCHANGE

A recent development in exchanging is the delayed exchange. In delayed exchange, one party gives up property for a dollar amount in property to be selected by the other party within a stated period of time. As an example, suppose I wanted a property you had, but because of tax reasons you did not want to sell it. You might, however, agree to transfer the property to me now in exchange for $100,000 worth of property which you are to select within six months.

While the Ninth Circuit Court of Appeals has allowed delayed exchanges as tax-free exchanges, attorneys and CPAs differ in their attitude toward these delayed exchanges. Many believe they will be disallowed in other jurisdictions. The Ninth Circuit Court of Appeals is generally considered more liberal than most, and its decisions may not be what is finally recognized as the proper interpretation of the law. Delayed exchanges should be entered into only with legal counsel. The structuring of a delayed exchange can be critical as far as the tax consequences are concerned. Personally, I think delayed exchanges should be avoided.

SOCIETY OF EXCHANGE COUNSELORS

If you are interested in exchanging property, I recommend you contact a member of the Society of Exchange Counselors, a small organization of exchange specialists who have demonstrated their ability and knowledge. When you give an exchange listing, you should realize you are not agreeing to any exchange unless you are willing to accept the property offered.

You should fully explain to the exchanger what you wish to accomplish and why. Through exchange meetings held locally, regionally and nationally, members arrange exchanges involving hundreds of pieces of property of every imaginable type. Exchangers believe there is no bad property, just unwanted property.

For information about the Society of Exchange Counselors, as well as members in your area, write:

Society of Exchange Counselors
P.O. Box 41964
Sacramento, CA 95841

Endeavor vigorously to increase your property.

—Horace

12

Optioning Your Way To Success

Besides making a profit on what you own, by means of an option you can make a profit on property you do not own. An option gives you the positive right to purchase property at an agreed price and terms for a stated period of time. If you want the property, you can exercise your option and buy it; if you decide you don't wish to buy it, you don't have to. By failing to exercise the option, you only lose the price you paid for the option. An option allows you to take advantage of a favorable situation even though you may lack the capital to purchase the property.

CONSIDERATION

In order to have a valid option, the optionee (potential buyer) must actually give consideration to the optionor (owner). Consideration is anything of value; while usually money, it could be any item or right having value. It is not enough to merely state in the option that it is given for consideration; the consideration must actually change hands.

ADVANTAGES TO OPTIONS

An option provides the optionee with fantastic leverage. Just a few dollars can give you rights to very expensive property. As the optionee you should endeavor to obtain an option for the longest term and the lowest consideration possible. Of course, you also want the option to provide as favorable sales terms as possible.

If a property has a high vacancy rate or other problems, owners are often anxious to sell. If the owners have been unable to find a buyer, they could be very receptive to an option at a reasonable price. While real estate profession-als frequently talk in terms of an option amount related to the purchase price, such as 5 percent of the price for a six-month option, don't worry about formulas. You are dealing with people who are interested in selling their property. For an option you should pay the minimum amount necessary. The option price is real risk capital because, if the option is not exercised, the price will be lost.

I know of one case in which a person gave an owner a used outboard motor worth perhaps $500 for a three-month option to buy timber land for $750,000. The price for the option was less than one-tenth of 1 percent of the purchase price. The optionee was able to tie up property of great value with no cash outlay.

Once the owner has agreed to an option, you should try for an option to extend the option for a period of time at a payment of a like sum of money. As an example, instead of paying $500 for a three-month option, you now also would have the right during the three-month period to extend the option for another three months by paying an additional $500. This extension agree-ment doesn't cost you anything to negotiate. It only costs you if you wish to exercise the extension. If you have a deal going but not firm, you will find the extension agreement very valuable.

Don't just go out looking to buy options; they should be procured selectively. If you feel a property can be turned at a profit, an option is the logical move for an investor with limited capital. The downside risk of buying an option is limited to the price paid for the option. The upside profit potential is limited only by what a buyer will pay.

OPTIONS ON COMMERCIAL AND INDUSTRIAL PROPERTY

Options to buy vacant commercial or industrial property can be extremely valuable. If you can procure good tenants at long-term leases, the property becomes readily saleable to investors.

I know of a case in which the optionee found a national company tenant who wanted a twenty-year lease. Based on the financial strength of the tenant and the agreed rental, the optionee was able to borrow enough on the building not only to cover its full purchase price, but actually to have cash left over. What happened was that the lease so increased the value of the property that a loan at 70 percent of the appraised value was actually more than 100 percent of what the optionee was required to pay as the purchase price.

Good tenants not only make a property more saleable, they can increase the value to the point where you as optionee may be able to buy the property without using any of your own money.

By meeting with national franchisors you can get to know their requirements. If you can get an option on property which satisfies their needs, a profit is likely. The franchisors normally are happy to work with anyone who can help them obtain desirable locations. Some optionees, once they obtain what they consider a good option, will try to put together a group of investors to buy the property as a limited partnership. The optionee will act as the general partner, taking a piece of the investment for his or her efforts.

With an option it is possible to list the property for sale with a real estate agent. Even after paying a commission, a good profit is possible when the option price is right.

Often owners who don't have their property officially for sale will give options at a price they consider desirable. While the price may be high at present, if the option is for a long enough period of time, such as one year, inflation as well as specific economic factors of an area can turn it into a bargain by the time an option is exercised. For instance, raw land options are usually readily obtainable. Slight changes in the economy can have great effects on land value.

I know several investors who buy options in the area of any large new development as soon as announcements are made. While they usually set purchase prices several times what the property was worth before the announcement, these premium prices often rapidly become bargains. For example, when Atlantic City made gambling legal, some investors purchased options for what many considered ridiculous sale prices. The owners felt that they would be instant millionaires if the options were exercised and were eager to accept the option consideration. While the optionors became millionaires, so did the optionees. Although we don't often have a situation like Atlantic City, a new college, hospital, factory or shopping center all offer potential for option profit.

ZONING CHANGES INCREASING PROPERTY VALUE

I know of one investor who buys options on improved and unimproved property, but only when he feels the zoning can be changed. After obtaining the option, he will try to obtain zoning changes which will increase the value of the property. If the investor is successful, he then exercises the option. Zoning changes can make a difference in value.

Another investor I know tied up 120 acres of land for one year with a $5,000 option price. He then obtained the zoning as well as building permits for a 600-space mobile home park. This investor sold the option with permits for $250,000 and regretted it later. He sold it far too cheaply.

TENANT OPTIONS

In past years landlords frequently gave options to purchase to their tenants as part of the lease. The option price was usually set quite high. The landlords never expected values to climb as they have in the past few years. Often these options were for long periods of time such as five years. Tenants with leases such as this are in a position to take advantage of a bargain.

BUYING OTHER PEOPLE'S OPTIONS

Recently, while buying furniture, I asked the owner of the store if he owned the building. He said no but he had an option to buy it. I then asked if he was going to exercise the option. He informed me that he could not afford to take the money out of the business to meet the downpayment requirements. When I found out the option price, I offered to buy his option for $10,000. He accepted, and I am now in the process of buying a building for $130,000 which I feel is worth in excess of $200,000.

Even though I have never heard of anyone doing it, I believe it could be possible to purchase some good options by advertising "Tenants—Residential, Commercial, Industrial. I will pay you cash for your option to purchase." It might even pay to knock on doors or canvass by telephone for options. You would want to concentrate on commercial tenants as options are more common in these leases. There must be thousands of good options expiring without being exercised, but it would take legwork to find them.

Before you buy an existing option from a tenant, you should check with an attorney. There could be legal problems as to the transferability of the option. If transferring the option creates problems, it is possible to have a double escrow in which the tenant takes title and immediately transfers it to you.

When you make an offer to an owner for an option, I recommend you do it in writing. It would be wise to have an attorney prepare your first option, although there are option forms available at many stationery stores. The problem with preprinted forms is that they seldom include everything you want and may include things you don't want.

GRANTING OPTIONS

While as a buyer you may want to buy options because of the huge profit potential they offer, you should be hesitant about giving options as an owner for any longer than a few months. Just as when buying an option you considered possible changes which would increase the value, consider the possibility of something happening of which you are not aware. You should check to see if other owners in the immediate neighborhood have been offered money for options. If they have, then the optionee knows of or hopes for something of which you are not aware.

If you as an owner are going to give an option for a long period of time such as one year, I suggest that the option be tied to the Consumer Price Index so that inflation does not lower your real price.

OPTIONS TO RENT

Options to rent open up an entirely different area of profit potential. For these options you should look for rentals that have been vacant for some time. Usually these will be stores, offices or industrial properties. While sale options are frequently difficult to obtain, options to rent are easy to obtain for periods of from thirty to sixty days. Owners often desperately want a tenant and are willing to tie up the property for one or two months at a very low option fee.

I recommend you try for a one-year option to rent at as low a price as you can negotiate, plus options to renew for two five-year periods at stated rentals. The option should also allow you the right to sublet or assign the lease. After the owner has agreed to the option, I suggest you ask that an option to purchase be included during the first year at an agreed price. In this way a purchase option can often be obtained without additional consideration.

Once you have the option to lease, get to work looking for a tenant at a higher rental than you have agreed to pay. If you obtain a tenant, you have made the rental difference between what your tenant will pay you and the rent you have agreed to pay. In some cases this profit can be substantial. It can increase each year if you are paying a flat rental figure and your tenant's rental increases with the Consumer Price Index.

As previously mentioned, one very effective way to find tenants is to go through the yellow pages and look for categories of tenants who could use your space. Simply call each listing in each applicable category and ask if the business can use the location at a desirable rent. Although this method is time-consuming, you will not only rent property, you will also get many leads for people looking for other properties as well. While calling on the phone eight hours a day, day after day, is tedious work, it can pay off.

There are people who look for shopping centers and office buildings in trouble. They will offer to lease all the vacant space on a long-term lease at an extremely low rental, usually just enough to allow the owner to make the payments on the mortgage. If an owner is desperate, he or she will accept this type of arrangement. The lessee is not a thief, since he or she is taking a high-risk gamble. While no one else could lease this space or keep it leased, the lessee is betting that he or she will be successful in subleasing it. This type of arrangement requires a strong financial position as well as a great deal of courage and ability.

RIGHT OF FIRST REFUSAL

If you lease, you should of course try for a purchase option, which can be frosting on the cake in the form of another profit potential. However, if you are the landlord, you should resist giving a tenant a purchase option. You can, however, safely give a right of first refusal. Under a right of first refusal, the tenant does not have the right to buy if you don't want to sell. However, if you want to sell to a buyer, before you can complete the sale you must go to the tenant and offer the property to the tenant at the same price and terms you are willing to accept from the other buyer. You are not really giving up very much when you give a right of first refusal.

Options, if used properly, can result in great profit. They avoid the downpayment and risk of a purchase while offering profit potential by leasing or sale. Ownership isn't necessary for profit; only control is.

13

Special Situations

IMAGINATION AND DETERMINATION PAY OFF

In 1948 a very successful attorney accompanied a friend to a boat show and fell in love with one of the larger yachts on display. It has been said that the difference between a man and a boy is only in the price of his toys. Well, the attorney purchased his toy that day. The next day was not as pleasant when he discovered that all the public moorings in the area had long waiting lists. About the only way to get a public mooring was to buy a boat already tied up at a mooring, which wouldn't help him as he had already purchased a boat. A number of the private yacht clubs had moorings available but required club membership. In those days, memberships were 100 percent Gentile; a Jewish attorney could forget about even applying. One of his friends in the real estate business told him that he could help temporarily. The friend had listed for sale a coal yard on the river not too far from the ocean. The yard had a dock and since it was closed, the real estate agent thought he could arrange with the owners for temporary docking privileges.

The attorney went to look at the dock. Although located in a run-down commercial and industrial area, the yard had five acres and over 600 feet on the river. The existing dock was for large ships, so it was more than ample for his yacht. The attorney knew that this was only temporary; he wanted some place to keep his boat permanently. He offered $50,000 cash for the old coal yard. The offer, while low, was accepted. This acceptance set in motion an amazing series of negotiations.

The attorney thought that if he had so much trouble getting a place to keep a boat, other people also would need moorage space. Before the sale of the coal yard was completed, he had an architect draw up preliminary plans for a private marina.

With the preliminary sketches he contacted the major oil companies to see if they would be interested in handling the fuel sales at his marina. This was at a time when oil companies were producing more than they could sell. There was fierce competition for retail sales. Oil companies built new service stations not as much for profit as to have an outlet for their products. As could be expected, a number of companies were very interested, since large boats use tremendous quantities of fuel. The attorney not only wanted the oil companies to build their own facilities, he also wanted a percentage of the gross as rent coupled with a minimum rent. In addition, he insisted on $50,000 being paid in advance rent when the facility opened. Several of the oil companies backed off at this demand, but one agreed to it and was given the oil and gas franchises.

Next, the attorney approached a firm that ran other mooring facilities. This firm agreed to construct the yacht slips and a boat ramp and to split all mooring fees fifty-fifty with the attorney. The company also would set up boat hoists to handle winter storage. The attorney was also to receive a percentage of this business as well as a percentage of any repair business. This agreement was for twenty years, after which all improvements became the property of the attorney.

Then the attorney looked into finding an excellent club manager. He hired away the manager of one of the exclusive clubs with a generous contract. The manager was given the job of selling 300 full memberships for $1,500 each, which included the right to rent a boat slip. These memberships were all sold within three months. Incidentally, all memberships were sold without racial or religious restrictions. Social memberships were sold for $500 each. These memberships allowed the members to use launching facilities as well as to rent temporary dock space on a daily basis. After the memberships were sold, the manager's job was to handle special social functions and to oversee the entire operation.

A magnificent club house was constructed, using the membership money collected. A restaurant operator put in the restaurant and bar equipment and agreed to pay a minimum rental plus a percentage of the gross.

In less than one year from the date he had first seen this rundown coal yard, the attorney had transformed it into a quality yacht club. What is amazing is that not only did he build it without leaving any of his own money in it, but the attorney now owned the entire property free and clear of all liens. By recognizing a need and planning a solution, he had creatively put together one of the finest operations of its kind. This unusual situation shows what can be accomplished with faith in your own ability and the guts to go ahead. There may not be yacht club possibilities such as this in your area, but there are always areas where imagination can lead to great profit.

PROBLEM PROPERTIES HAVE POTENTIAL

One of the most interesting problem properties I know of was a house of ill repute built in the late 1930s. The building, of log construction, was in a northern resort area. It was set far back from the highway on a large parcel of land, making it quite isolated. Downstairs was one large room which originally served as a bar and dance area. It also had bathroom facilities. Upstairs were twelve extremely tiny rooms off a central hall. Each room had a sink and a window. There were also bathroom facilities on the second floor. The building had a succession of owners. Several restaurants had gone broke on the premises and the building had been vacant for several years. The house was finally listed with an imaginative broker. She wrote several hundred letters to psychologists in nearby cities and also advertised in a psychology magazine. She sold the building to a psychologist who was engaged in various types of encounter groups. The property was ideally suited for groups such as this or for training purposes. When real estate has a problem, problem solving can offer financial rewards.

Many small communities have serious unemployment problems. Some of these communities have set up industrial development corporations which have sold low-interest bonds to raise funds to attract industry. Many communities will build buildings for employers and rent them at very low rentals. Others even make loans to firms that will come into the community. Unfortunately, in the desire for employers, many communities have built structures for firms with financial problems. The result has been that many of these development groups have vacant buildings. These situations offer great potential for problem solvers. Options can often be obtained on these completed structures at extremely low rentals if the use will provide an agreed number of jobs. If you can find firms that would benefit by moving to the area, you can make a profit by the rental differential and solve a community need.

MOBILE HOME UNITS

A couple in California lived in a ten-by-fifty-foot mobile home. They decided they wanted a double-wide unit. The couple discovered that they could only get about $1,500 by selling their unit and, although they could get several thousand dollars on a trade-in, they could actually buy the double-wide they wanted for almost the same amount if they had no trade-in. This couple purchased their double-wide unit but kept their old mobile home, moving it to a fairly rough family park where space rentals at the time were only $40 a month. They rented their old coach for $130 a month furnished. In fact, they had a great many calls on the rental ad. The couple did some figuring and realized that they were clearing $90 a month on their old coach, or $1,080 each year. In a year and a half this would give them as much as they would have received by selling the unit. They visited several mobile home dealers and said they were interested in buying for up to $2,000 ten-foot and twelve-foot-wide units that had been taken in on trade. The couple wanted the dealers to finance the units at 10 percent down on four-year loans. Several of the dealers were interested, since very few buyers wanted old single-wide units.

The couple then made deals with several older mobile home parks having vacancies. While better parks wouldn't take in an old single-wide, many of the smaller parks with vacancies would do so. In one park they rented ten spaces for $25 each per month and were able to get a five-year lease at that rent. In a little over one year both were able to quit their jobs to handle their mobile home rentals full time.

This couple saw a need and a means to fulfill it. Unlike many people who just talk, they acted. Now they own well over 100 rental units and, while not prestige property, it is highly profitable.

FACTORIES

Because of manufacturing inefficiencies, many multistory factories have become obsolete. They have often been sold at very low prices and excellent terms because their use has been limited. Some people with imagination have turned these structures into productive buildings. Some have been leased to crafts people who each rent space. This draws many tourists as well as local shoppers to the buildings. Some factories have been converted to large nightclubs, restaurants, skating rinks and even legitimate theaters. Some have been converted to apartments. Conversion costs are high, but may still be far below the cost of building new units.

CREATIVE CONVERSION OF OLDER PROPERTIES

For many years consumers have had the idea that new means better. Today more and more people are thinking back to a time before our plastic age when things were simpler and didn't break. We have seen a fantastic demand not only for antiques but also for goods produced only twenty to thirty years ago. The older the car a person drives today, the more fashionable that person is.

Old mansions were in years past frequently converted to rooming houses. Today many of these old mansions are being reconverted to another use, fashionable offices. Many firms like the uniqueness and charm these buildings provide. A great number of buildings which were formerly modernized are now being restored to their original appearance. While new may be good, for many people old is better.

Old office buildings with iron railings and open iron elevator cages were being ripped down in the 1950s and 1960s to make room for new glass towers. Today many old buildings have regained their former luster and command premium rentals. Attorneys, accountants and other professionals like the solid image these structures provide. A building should have a basically sound structure and classic lines if you are considering restoration. In the future we can expect even greater value to be placed on the styles and craftsmanship of past generations.

Old schoolhouses and train depots can at times be purchased at very low prices. They offer exceptional possibilities for shops, restaurants and even apartments.

> Some years ago I purchased a huge old home from the state. The state had acquired the home when they foreclosed on a state veterans loan. I paid $7,500 with $500 down and the balance at $75 per month, including interest at 5 percent. The home had been built in a small town by a doctor over seventy-five years earlier. The property had some lake frontage on a lake known for its lousy fishing. At the time I purchased the house I didn't know who would want it, but I felt I could do something with it. The oak woodwork and paneling were fantastic. The home had a huge sunroom along one side. All the rooms were large. The only real problem was that it had sixteen rooms, three stories and a basement but only one bath. I spent about $500 cleaning the building out. I made some plaster repairs and mowed the huge lawn. I placed an ad in the *Chicago Tribune* (Chicago was about 250 miles away), advertising it as ideal for an artist, describing the large sunroom as a studio. I sold the property for $16,000 to a sculptor who loved having so much space.

THE VALUE OF OLD FURNITURE

Incidentally, in cleaning out the basement and attic of that huge old home, I received my indoctrination into the world of antiques. I mentioned to a friend that the attic and basement of the place were loaded with old junk. My friend was an antique buff and drove up to look at the property with me. My friend agreed to clean out the attic and basement, throwing out the real junk and selling what was saleable. In exchange I agreed to let my friend have several old bureaus. Over the next few months my friend gave me a number of checks totaling over $1,000. After this experience I started looking differently at the "junk" left in old buildings.

Since then I have purchased many older furnished homes and apartments. In several cases the resale of the furniture has gone a long way toward returning my downpayment. Those old 1912 Sears oak chests are now regarded as valuable antiques. In the basement of one apartment building I found six old oak iceboxes, which I sold for $200 each.

> A close friend purchased a lake cottage which had been part of a resort. On the same lot as his cottage was an old four-car garage, in bad shape but full of old wicker porch furniture. The sale of these pieces more than doubled his downpayment.

TREE AND TIMBER VALUE

If you should find a property with a fine old black walnut tree on it, this would be like finding gold. One tree, depending on size and configuration, could be worth up to $10,000. There is a ready market for veneer quality logs from plywood manufacturers. I heard of one country home which was sold with nine such trees on the front lawn. The purchaser harvested his lawn and received more than the price of the entire property from the sale of the trees.

A fishing companion of mine purchased a heavily wooded lot of several acres for $5,000. In building his home he had to clear away a number of trees over 100 years old. Rather than pay for their removal, he called in a logger who not only cleared the site but also paid him almost $3,000.

Not all timber is valuable but much of it is. People with smaller parcels of land often fail to consider the fact that there may be value in the timber.

HOW A PROPERTY CAN RISE IN VALUE

A few years ago a nationally known entertainer donated eighty acres for a community medical center. The land given was located quite a distance from any populated area. In fact, at the time, it looked as if a worse location could not have been found. With the entertainer helping with the fundraising, the medical center was completed. Land prices in the area rose sharply as new developments were started. People who purchased land when the center was first announced made tremendous profits. The person who profited most was the entertainer himself. The land given was only a small part of a much larger parcel he owned. The rest of his property has gone up from twenty to fifty times what it was worth before he made his charitable gift.

Being in close proximity to a major hospital, college or similar institution will of course help property values. While I don't know in this case if the results of the gift were considered at the time the gift was made, you can see that it might pay to give away some land for a particular purpose if that purpose will aid the area and if you retain the surrounding land. In addition, a charitable gift, of course, means a tax deduction.

MEETING SPECIAL GROUP NEEDS

Several apartment buildings in the Sunbelt have in recent years gone "clothing optional." These are apartment units with private interior courts, usually with a pool. Dedicated nudists have filled up the units at premium rents. In the Los Angeles area these units command rents about 50 percent higher than otherwise comparable units.

An apartment building owner I know is seriously considering turning his apartment complex into units aimed at meeting the needs of the gay community. The owner, who is gay himself, claims neighbors frequently make gays feel uncomfortable. He feels gays will pay a premium rent for units in his complex and intends to test his idea with ads in gay publications, evaluating the responses. One possible problem the owner could face is that he might be in violation of antidiscrimination laws if he discriminates against prospective tenants by sex and marital status.

STUDENT HOUSING

The conversion of apartments to student housing can be lucrative. It is not unusual for a unit which formerly rented for $350 a month to bring in $150 from each of four students. You should remember that student housing is often only rented nine to ten months per year. This type of rental usually means extremely high maintenance costs.

HIGHWAY REROUTING

When highways change routes, there is often panic among owners of property on the former route, especially motel owners. Motels in such circumstances can often be purchased at very low prices. They can be converted to a number of uses, including nursing homes, private schools, retarded care facilities and even apartments for singles.

STORAGE UNITS

Miniwarehouses and storage yards are being built across the country. They are fulfilling a real need.

One large storage yard owner didn't buy the land. He went to a landowner who owned choice highway property and offered to lease the property for seven years. Since many owners intend to let their land appreciate, the chance for even a modest income during the holding period is like found money. The operator leased a large parcel, installed cyclone-type steel fencing with barbed wire on top and a gate. The lot now has over 300 boats, recreational vehicles and construction equipment stored at from ten to twenty dollars per month.

A similar arrangement was made by a woman who leased several acres of land on a twenty-year lease and put a miniwarehouse on it. She used prefabricated steel units. Financing was arranged for her by the manufacturer of the steel buildings. She ended up with 140 rental units with a $50,000 investment.

MAKING MONEY OFF THE LAND

It is possible to make money from land while it is being held for appreciation. Some states pay small amounts per acre if the land is declared a game preserve. States also give a property tax break if land is turned into forest. Some owners have planted fir trees, getting the trees at nominal costs from the state. These owners also take whatever tax benefits are available. Before developing their land, they harvest their crop of Christmas trees.

REDEVELOPMENT AND HIGHWAY CONSTRUCTION

These often create situations in which good structures are available at very low prices. However, such structures must be moved. In planning to buy such a building, you must first consider local regulations. Can the structure be put on a lot in the area? Besides the zoning, the covenants, conditions and restrictions could prohibit it. In addition to the initial cost of the building, you should consider moving costs, cost of a lot, foundation expense, water and sewage costs, electrical hookups, driveways and walks and even insurance for the move. There will be additional electrical expenses for a basement, and some new duct work could be required. Building codes could require a new hot water heater or a new furnace. Despite all these costs, moving a structure can be a valuable investment. Some larger buildings are actually cut into pieces to be moved.

The uses and development of real estate are limited only by your imagination. These examples are not given to show you what to do so much as to show you that you should be flexible in understanding and solving real estate problems. And remember that finding solutions to problems is meaningless unless you act upon them.

Love people and use things; don't love things and use people.
—*Anonymous*

14

Managing Your Property

Bernard Baruch gave a four-word plan for riches: "Buy low, sell high." It sounds simple, but what do you do with the property between the time you acquire it and the time you dispose of it? What you do will be an important factor in what the property will bring at a sale.

Property management includes a very broad area of planning and decision making. It involves goal setting, improvements, changes in use, tenant selection, rent collections, policies and procedures and a great deal more. Property management requires skills in management, bookkeeping and interpersonal relationships.

Good real estate management will maximize the net return. A higher net means a greater value. A property should be analyzed in terms of what use and type of tenant will provide the greatest return, and a plan should be devised to achieve that goal. Costs reported by the former owner should be analyzed as to necessity and accuracy. Realistic operational and improvement costs should be estimated.

PRINCIPLE OF CONTRIBUTION

In planning, economics must be considered. I know of owners who have spent more money on improvements than could possibly be recouped in increased revenues. When considering improvements, you should consider the principle of contribution. Ask yourself how much the improvements will contribute to the net income. I use a ratio of six in my personal planning. If I do not believe the improvement costs will be paid for within six years by an increased net income, I will not make the improvements. I feel I can use my money better for other purposes.

A friend of mine purchased a small office building. All the tenants had several years left on their leases. After purchasing the building, my friend did extensive landscaping of an interior court. He also

127

repaved the walks with red brick and installed a very large fountain. His costs for this work amounted to about $20,000. At first glance these improvements appeared unnecessary, but these were his reasons for the improvements:

1. Tenant satisfaction. A happy tenant is likely to remain, thus reducing the vacancy factor. When leases expire, my friend will be competing with many new buildings. He does not want to lose his tenants. Increased net can be in the form of a reduced vacancy factor as well as higher rents.
2. Property appreciation. When the property is eventually sold, the improvements will help sell the building and should increase the sale price.
3. Tax benefits. Part of the work was repair, which can be written off completely as an expense in the year of the repair. The work which was an improvement can be depreciated over the life of the improvement. Uncle Sam, therefore, will pick up the tab for half the expenses because of my friend's tax bracket.

UNDERSTANDING PROPERTY MANAGEMENT

I recommend that every investor understand property management. There is no better way to learn than to manage your own property. While there are some excellent management firms, professional management will not provide you with an education in property management. There is no substitute for personal involvement. The management experience you gain will be invaluable to you in making future investment decisions.

LEASES

Before a purchase you will want to see all current leases. At the time of closing you will want to make sure all lease deposits are turned over to you. Lease deposits can actually help you purchase a property.

I once handled the sale of a forty-unit apartment building for which the downpayment was to be $50,000. All the tenants had $200 security deposits, which were turned over to the seller at time of closing. The net effect of receiving this $8,000 was that the buyer had to come up with only $42,000 at the time of closing.

RENTS

Rents are prorated as of the day of closing but are usually paid in advance. Therefore, unless the rents are all due on the date of closing, the buyer is entitled to that portion of the rent which has been prepaid beyond the day of closing. For example, assume the rent is $200 and is paid on the first of the month. If the closing is on the fifteenth, then the seller would have collected rent for fifteen days after the sale. The seller must pay the buyer for these fifteen days. In this case the payment would be $100. Prorations are normally based on a thirty-day month.

INSURANCE NEEDS

Before the sale is completed, you should have considered your insurance needs. While existing policies usually can be assumed, they may not be adequate for your needs. You will probably desire an extended coverage policy which covers replacement of real and personal property without deductions for depreciation. You will want a high liability coverage, as well as coverage for vandalism, accidents and so forth. You may also want plate glass coverage. Rental interruption coverage will reimburse you for lost rents because of a casualty loss. If you are taking over maintenance employees with the property, you should consider the necessity of workmen's compensation coverage as well as unemployment compensation. I suggest you review the property fully with your insurance broker prior to closing the transaction.

ONCE THE PROPERTY IS YOURS

At closing, the former owner should turn over a complete set of keys to you. You can require this to be done in your purchase offer. Nothing is more annoying than having tenants move out and take the only keys with them. I keep a key file with a complete duplicate set of keys for all my properties.

RENT INCREASES AND PROPERTY IMPROVEMENTS

As soon as the property is yours, you should immediately notify all tenants that you are the new owner and that all future rents are to be paid to you. Often units have below-market rentals. Tenants usually know when they have been getting a good deal. They will in these cases be expecting a rent increase.

Before I raise rents, I try to make some sort of repair or improvement in order to show the tenants that I care about the property and will keep it up. It improves the landlord-tenant relationship if the tenants feel they are getting something for their increased rent.

TENANT PROBLEMS

Often property is sold because an owner has had problems with tenants. I visit such tenants personally and listen to their problems. I believe in complete honesty: I will tell the tenant either that corrections will be made and when, or if not, why not. Procrastination only causes further problems. If the tenants say they will move, I write out a statement and ask them to sign it. If I feel a residential tenant will be a problem, I usually prefer that he or she leave. I will normally allow a problem tenant to break a lease without any penalty.

While most people are really great, I, unlike Will Rogers, have met people I didn't like. Some people are just unreasonable. They expect more than is reasonable of a landlord and complain about everything imaginable. You must explain to people that in apartment living they must expect to give up some of the quiet and privacy of a single-family dwelling. Nevertheless, I will usually do all I feasibly can to satisfy tenant problems.

Occasionally a tenant will go on a rent strike, saying that he or she will not pay the rent until something is done. I counter by immediately starting eviction proceedings. I will not submit to extortion of this type. From experience I have found that in most cases this tenant action is simply a means to avoid paying the rent. The tenant really hopes that you will take several months to make the demanded repairs, thus giving several months' free rent.

In managing property you will come across people who will try to take advantage of you. When a tenant cannot pay rent on time or the rent check bounces, I want to know why and when I can expect a check. I have the tenant agree on a date of payment and then send the tenant a letter showing this agreement. If the tenant does not pay as agreed, I then start eviction proceedings. I don't believe in giving a third chance.

Tenants will frequently try several ploys to gain time in paying their rent. The two most common are the wrong checks with the letter (you receive a check for a charge card while the credit company receives your check) and unsigned checks. You must also be alert for the tenant who wants to go on a forty-day month. The tenant will be ten days late with the first check and then send a check every forty days, thus falling farther and farther behind in his or her rent. In four years the tenant will be one year behind. Some owners won't evict since they continue to get checks on a regular basis, and the tenant will promise to make it up. The owner hopes this is true and is afraid that the tenant, if evicted, will never pay.

There are all kinds of deadbeats. I had one gentleman give a small deposit on a quality unit and tell me he would send me a money order for three months' rent plus the security deposit before he moved into the city. While I told him I required only the deposit plus one month's rent, he said that he traveled a great deal and didn't like

to bother with a check each month but always liked to pay several months in advance. I didn't get the money order, but the gentleman showed up for the keys. He acted surprised that I hadn't received the money order and asked his wife if she had a receipt for it, which she found after some digging in her purse. The receipt was for well over $1,000, which was the exact amount of three months' rent plus security and key deposits, less the deposit they had previously made. The husband said that they had cash and showed me a large wad of bills. He explained, however, that this was for the movers who were due in a matter of hours. Well, I gave them the keys, expecting to receive the money order in a few days. I did not receive it, so my tenants said they would put a tracer on it with the post office. For three months we looked for that lost money order. When the fourth month's rent was due, the tenants stopped by my office to tell me they would be a little late as they had sold some property back east and would be getting $50,000 in just a few days. The gentleman also wanted to know if I would sell him the apartment building. Luckily I finally realized I had been taken. I ran a credit check in the city these people had moved from and discovered they were masters of not paying bills. They had pulled similar stunts with a previous landlord. Apparently they had purchased a money order and then filled in the payee as themselves. They cashed it but had the original purchase receipt to show me. If I had believed their purchase strategy, the couple would have received several more months free rent. There are not many people such as this, but they do exist. My mistake was in not checking on them immediately.

EVICTIONS COST MONEY

As an owner, I cannot take all the burdens of my tenants on my shoulders. If I allowed tenants with difficulty to remain without paying rent, I would soon be without property. I direct tenants with problems to the appropriate social agency. I have also found tenants rentals which they could afford and have moved them to their new apartments. Actually this makes sense from an economic as well as a human standpoint. The cost of moving could very well be less than the cost and time involved in an eviction.

At one time I owned and managed a great number of low-rent units. Tenant problems were quite common. I often found it was cheaper to pay a tenant to move than to evict. For instance, if a tenant has problems and it appears that rent collections would be difficult or impossible, I might agree to give the tenant $100 or more when he or she turned over the key to me. If I had evicted, I would be faced with the legal expense, a rental loss during the eviction and possible property damage. I have actually had vindictive tenants leave property in shambles. However, when they know I am going to inspect the property before paying them, the property is usually clean with the exception of normal wear and tear.

IF EVICTION OCCURS

In most states you can handle evictions without an attorney. The clerk of your local county court should be able to show you what papers to use and how to fill them out. Normally, the first step is a notice to quit or pay rent (usually a three-day notice). If the tenant doesn't leave after this notice, and he or she seldom does, it is followed by an unlawful detainer action, which is the court eviction proceedings. The court will usually give the tenant several weeks to leave. If the tenant does not leave, you can get the sheriff to move the tenant, although you will probably pay the moving expense.

Never evict a tenant in December. Courts and the community will regard you as a Scrooge for pre-Christmas evictions.

If a property owner evicts residential tenants for a condominium conversion or a change in use, I feel that the owner has a moral obligation to his or her tenants beyond the bare legal notices to vacate that are required by law. In cases in which I have evicted tenants, I have actively sought other units that would meet their needs, as well as helped in relocation costs. Moral values are not incompatible with profit.

DECIDING ON RENTAL RATES

A vacant unit will give you an opportunity to reassess your rents. You should consider the law of supply and demand. If there are few vacancies in an area, a higher rental might be feasible. You should survey the rental market. You are not interested in what similar units are renting at but what owners are asking for similar vacant units. Your vacant unit is not competing with all similar units, only with the vacant ones.

In analyzing competing units, you should consider the following:

1. Size of unit
2. Condition of unit
3. Appearance of building
4. Security of building
5. Parking or garage
6. Utilities furnished
7. Neighborhood
8. Transportation
9. Elevator or walk-up
10. Children allowed
11. Pets allowed

If you set too high a rent, you can expect an increase in your vacancy factor. An increase in vacancies can more than offset a rent increase and result in a net loss. As an example, suppose you had ten units, each renting for $200 per month, or a total monthly rental income of $2,000. If you raised the rents 10 percent, you would now have a $2,200 per month gross. Assume this increase resulted in a 10 percent vacancy factor. You would now have only a $1,980 gross, or a decline in total gross of 1 percent. Therefore, you must carefully evaluate the effect of a rent increase on your vacancy factor.

If you rent one unit at a higher rate, you must raise the other units also, although you may have to wait until leases expire to do so. Rents should be consistent. People don't mind paying a fair rental unless they find your other tenants are paying less than they are. You might feel that tenants will resist a rent increase beyond a particular price, such as $500. An alternative without quite the stigma of a rent increase is a charge for services previously provided. For example, charges for cable TV, water, trash removal or even parking spaces are equivalent to a rent increase but are regarded slightly more favorably.

Some cities have rent controls. One way to still get a rent increase is to furnish the unit when it becomes vacant. By changing the nature of the unit, you can sometimes charge a higher rent.

CONDITION OF RENTAL UNIT

In periods when demand for housing exceeds the available supply, it is possible to rent a vacated unit without doing any work. Nevertheless, at the very least I will see that a unit is properly cleaned before it is rented. Tile floors should be stripped and waxed and rugs steam cleaned. Although all tenants are not neat and clean, they deserve to start out with a spotless unit. When a unit is vacant, it is a good time for minor upgrading such as new light fixtures or carpets. If the walls need it, they can be painted or wallpapered. I use wallpaper only in baths and dining areas and then a vinyl cloth paper which can be wiped clean. I use only a few standard colors for paint, so I can touch up walls rather than completely repainting. I use light colors, which make a unit appear both cleaner and larger. Some owners will provide the tenant with the paint, but I have found from sad experience that many people are completely inept. Therefore, I do not allow tenants to paint their own units.

Drapes and shades should be inspected and repaired, cleaned or replaced as needed. When drapes need to be replaced, I usually use inexpensive, light-colored, foam-backed drapes from Penney's or Sears, as I find that they clean well and are available in enough standard sizes to fit just about any window.

If the plaster is bad, I find it is easiest to cover it with inexpensive prefinished plywood paneling. If a ceiling is in bad shape, ceiling tile can be installed with a mastic.

When I upgrade a vacant unit, I like to add the following where needed:

1. New light fixtures in kitchen and bath.
2. A large mirrored medicine chest with a built-in light fixture.
3. A quality vinyl wallpaper on at least one wall in the bath.
4. A forty-inch wainscotting of a washable wallpaper topped with a molding strip in the dining area.
5. Several rows of ceramic tile behind the stove, applied with a special mastic.

The unit should be clean and free of vermin, and all appliances and utilities should sparkle and work properly. The unit must meet the minimum standards of providing protection from the elements; it does not need to be of a quality you would like for yourself. Don't substitute your tastes for the taste of others. By doing so, you can end up spending far more for upgrading than can ever be returned in increased rents. Remember that to many people your unit will be offering an improvement in their quality of life.

FURNISHED UNITS AND APPLIANCE AND FURNITURE STORAGE

In deciding if a unit should be furnished, you should analyze the market for furnished units. Generally, furnished units rent at premium rentals. However, tenancy for furnished units is usually shorter. Unless there is very strong demand, furnished units will have a much higher vacancy factor than unfurnished units.

When I managed a great number of residential units, I kept a double garage as a storeroom for furniture and appliances. I made deals with appliance dealers to buy their better used trade-ins. Once I purchased thirty fairly new refrigerators and stoves from a wrecker who was taking down an apartment building to make way for a freeway. I was occasionally able to buy a whole household of furniture at a relatively low price. I used the appliances to upgrade units and the furniture both to upgrade furnished units and to furnish additional units.

When I formerly managed some large unfurnished complexes, I would get inquiries on furnished units. I arranged a furniture package with a local furniture store and told prospective tenants that for a stated additional cost they could get a furnished unit and at the end of three years they would own the furniture. What we actually did was arrange for 100 percent financing of the furniture package, and the tenant would make two payments, one to me for rent and one to the finance company for the furniture.

FINDING TENANTS TO FILL VACANCIES

Over half of my rentals come from the cheapest method possible, a sign. I indicate on the for-rent sign if the unit is furnished or unfurnished. I also use newspaper classified ads to fill vacancies. If an ad doesn't bring much response, I change it. I advertise the high points. Negative points such as no pets can be explained later. An ad is merely a teaser to excite interest; it is not a rental agreement.

If you do not reside in your units, you will want to designate one tenant to show the units and ask for deposits. You don't want someone actually renting; all you want is a deposit which gives you the right to accept or reject. I have learned from my past mistakes that a prospective tenant may not be what he or she appears to be. I have the applicant for a rental fill out a questionnaire and then I verify the applicant's employment. Also, I get a credit check. (You may have to join a local credit bureau to do this.) A poor past credit history normally means a problem tenant.

You cannot discriminate in housing based on race under the Civil Rights Act of 1968. Many state acts prohibit discrimination based on handicaps, sex and marital status. Only a few years ago owners would not tolerate tenants "living in sin," while today this relationship may be protected by your state's laws.

One rule I do have about tenant selection is that I will not rent to a friend. If you have a close friend as a tenant, there is a great danger that your personal relationship will suffer. How, for example, would you go about evicting a close friend?

RENT COLLECTION PROBLEMS

As a rule, units that rent for lower amounts require more management effort than more expensive units. Units with lower rentals tend to be older and more crowded. They require more maintenance and greater renovation between tenants. Rent collection problems seem to increase inversely to the amount of rent charged.

With lower-income tenants, it is necessary to collect rents in person on the dates social security and welfare checks are received. Some owners who have a great deal of slum property actually have armed guards accompany them on collection days. They must carry a great deal of cash in order to cash checks. I personally will not own this type of property, as I am not willing to undergo the constant problems associated with slum properties.

ON-SITE APARTMENT MANAGERS

An owner can delegate many of the management tasks to a tenant. Reimbursement may be in the form of reduced rent, free rent or even free rent and a salary, depending on the duties required and the number of units involved. I like to use retired couples for this job since they have the time to devote to problems. An on-site manager also gets a psychic income in that he or she gets recognition from other tenants as a person in authority. I give my on-site manager calling cards with his or her name and the title "Property Management Officer."

You should carefully spell out the duties of your apartment manager. If your manager is to collect rents, you should consider a fidelity bond. I prefer my tenants mailing the rents directly to me. I notify the on-site manager if there is any problem with rent collection. The on-site manager's job, besides taking rental deposits and handling minor maintenance, is to solve tenant problems. Tenants sometimes expect the management to solve every person-ality conflict that comes up. I recommend to my managers that they try to have the parties work out their differences before becoming involved.

Each year I set a realistic budget for maintenance supplies and outside services. The manager knows the budget. If the manager cannot make a repair, he or she calls a particular plumber, electrician or other tradesperson with whom I do business. If the annual operation costs are below budget and the manager has not deferred maintenance to achieve this, I give a cash bonus to my manager of 25 percent of the amount we are below budget. What happens is that my managers are often able to make repairs they would have otherwise called in a tradesperson for. My little bonus system has saved money for me and helps keep my managers happy.

A number of years ago I hired a young couple to handle a large complex I managed. I felt the job was too much for an older couple. The night the couple moved in, three of the tenants called me complaining about my managers who had some friends over and were blasting rock music. My new managers left and I went back to older managers. I have had some of my best luck with retired military personnel. They are usually meticulous on the paperwork required and have excellent interpersonal skills.

COIN-OPERATED WASHERS AND DRYERS

These actually provide a profit in many units, especially in smaller units for singles. Some owners allow the managers to take this money for a petty cash fund. I don't recommend this procedure as the money will end up becoming part of the manager's compensation rather than cash to be used for materials.

Any petty cash fund should be unrelated to machine receipts and all funds should be accounted for. In a lower-income building I formerly managed, the coinboxes on the washers and dryers were constantly being broken open. I found that for this building it was cheaper to remove the coinboxes and provide the washers and dryers free of charge.

UTILITY COSTS

In these times of high utility costs you must consider ways to save. Outside lights should be on timers. Instead of 150-watt spotlights for outside lighting, I have gone to 12-volt, low-wattage systems. One apartment complex I recently visited has put in a meter for the tennis court lights. Fifty cents allows twenty minutes of lighting.

One way to cut lighting costs is to use fluorescent hall fixtures. Besides operating on lower wattage, they actually give more light. While ordinary light bulbs tend to disappear in halls, the fluorescent tubes seem to stay. Cutting heating and cooling costs can mean the difference between a profit and a loss. I presently don't own any units where I must supply heating and cooling, but there are many buildings with central systems. When utilities were cheap, it was an economical way to build. Many such buildings have now replaced central heating and cooling units with separate units so each tenant can pay his or her own bills. If this is not feasible, an owner of such a building should avoid long-term leases without a provision for increased rents based on utility costs.

With central heating and cooling, costs can be reduced in a number of ways. Locked thermostats and thermostats that change by a clock can mean significant savings. The days when landlords provided eighty-degree heat and seventy-degree cooling are part of the past.

Double insulation in crawl spaces or attics, weatherstripping and storm windows and doors all help. Planting a windbreak close to the building will also significantly reduce heat loss. Simple furnace modifications such as automatic flue controls will reduce the amount of heat going up the chimney.

REDUCING VACANCIES

In managing property, a dollar's savings in management costs is equivalent to another dollar in income, and every dollar in income means about ten to fifteen dollars in additional property value upon sale. Therefore, while you will want to maintain a property well in order to protect your investment, you don't want any unnecessary or wasted expenditure. You also want vacancies to be kept to a minimum.

You should insist that every tenant sign a lease. Even a tenant on a month-to-month tenancy should sign a lease, as the lease will clearly set forth the duties and obligations of the owner and the tenant.

Leases can reduce vacancies. The best rental periods are different in various areas of the country, but suppose in your area the best rental period is from May to September. By having all one-year leases expire on either May 1, June 1, July 1 or August 1, you would have fewer problems renting units if a tenant failed to renew the lease. You don't want leases to expire at periods when few people are moving. As an example, vacancies occurring on December 1 in many northern cities might be hard to fill unless there was a great shortage of housing.

A number of years ago I took over the management of a forty-seven-unit complex of two-bedroom apartments near a major airport. The units were in a quadrangle with a large inner court and a pool. Many of the units were furnished but were in rough shape. Units were rented by the week or month to families. The general rental period was fairly short, as people tended to rent the units only until they could find permanent accommodations. While rents were high for apartments, the units were usually at least one-third vacant. One problem with the property was its close proximity to the airport runway. The noise at times was deafening.

I prepared a management plan and cost estimates for the owner and obtained her concurrence. One of my first acts was to change the name of the building to "Airport Plaza," turning a negative location into a plus.

I started an immediate revitalization of the building. The exterior was painted and plantings were put in the interior courtyard. I added two Ping-Pong tables, several gas barbecues and a shuffleboard court, and I also increased the outside lighting.

We painted the vacant apartments and gave almost all the tenants thirty-day notices. I provided the tenants with a list of available units in the area and even allowed them to move early if they found a place, giving them a proportional rent rebate.

I furnished several apartments with high-style Danish modern furniture and modern prints on the walls. Our refurbishing included new lighting fixtures and in some cases new carpeting.

We had a grand opening party about forty-five days after I took over management. I visited all the airline desks at the airport and left loads of invitations for a champagne party. I asked that they invite all air crews, especially hostesses. The party was in the open court. I had a three-piece band and served several cases of California champagne. I rented six apartments that night. I had rentals based on the number of occupants. Two hundred and fifty dollars for two people. Three hundred and fifty for four people. This rental rate was almost twice what similar units were renting for. In the next two weeks I rented twenty units primarily to airline personnel. I next advertised in the newspaper. The ad began with, "Stewardesses Attention." It emphasized closeness to the airport as well as a beautiful pool to lounge at and the fun of an evening barbecue. This ad was effective in that it brought in the young men. When fully rented, the complex had about a fifty-fifty split between the sexes, with over 80 percent of the tenants under thirty years of age.

This happened several years before singles apartments had ever been heard of. We ended up with a noisy building always needing repairs, lots of parties, a zero vacancy factor and a long waiting list. All tenants were on one-year leases ending May 1, June 1, July 1 or August 1. The summer is the time to rent a pool apartment. Despite the horrendous maintenance expenses, the building showed a fantastic net income. What I did for these airport units was to analyze how I could get the maximum return from the units and then go for it.

PROPERTY DAMAGE BONDS AND OTHER SAFETY MEASURES

Of course, I required a property damage bond of all renters. This bond was equivalent to one month's rent. The purpose of such a bond is to pay for repair or replacement of furniture or for damages to the unit beyond normal wear and tear.

A property damage bond is better for an owner than collecting the last month's rent in advance. Rent collected in advance is considered accrued income and must be reported by the owner in the year it is collected for income tax purposes. However, a property damage bond is not taxable as income until it is forfeited, which may never happen. I also require a five-dollar key deposit. With a deposit this large, I very seldom fail to get keys returned.

You must be careful that you don't give too long a lease without safeguards to cover utility increases.

I know of an eight-year-old, 19,000-square-foot office building which can be purchased for less than $500,000. It has twelve years to go on a twenty-year lease to the state. The problem is that the owner pays all the utilities. While the lease has an escalation clause based on 50 percent of the annual increase in the Consumer Price Index, this increase is far less than the increases in fuel costs. When the lease was entered into, fuel oil was thirteen cents a gallon. The present owner has been losing a great deal of money each year and can only foresee additional losses.

USING THE HARD SELL

When you have a number of rentals to fill, you cannot take a lot of time for people to make up their minds. I use what many would consider a hard sell.

When I get a call on a rental, I give only bare information such as, "Yes, that is a lovely three-bedroom, first-floor unit in a newer building. The rent is $400 per month and a $400 property damage bond is required. It is available on a one-year lease. I can arrange to show it to you this afternoon at 2 P.M. Is that time convenient?" If there are any restrictions such as pets or children, I mention them at this time. The caller's response will either be that 2 P.M. is fine or that he or she can't make it, in which case I ask when he or she will be available. The caller thus sets the time to see the unit and I have an appointment. I usually average better than 50 percent showings from inquiries to my ads.

When showing the unit, I point out any features that are not obvious. It isn't necessary to tell someone, "This is the kitchen." I repeat the rental terms and state, "If you would like to apply for this rental, I will be happy to take your deposit. The customary deposit is $50, is that all right with you?" This straightforward approach works well. At the same time, I have the prospective tenant fill out a credit information card. I indicate that I will contact the prospective tenant within forty-eight hours. Usually I am able to complete employment and credit checks in a few hours. I then contact the prospective tenant and ask that he or she bring in the balance of the first month's rent and the property damage bond usually a week before occupancy.

FREE RENT IS BAD BUSINESS

Giving away rent is giving away profit. I don't believe in giving several months' free rent, a free color TV or free moving expenses to fill a unit, although all are done by some owners. I believe that if I make my units appear better than competing units, I won't have to give away freebies. I would rather spend the money in the unit than give it away as a rental inducement.

PROFESSIONAL PROPERTY MANAGERS

After you understand the day-to-day management problems, as well as management planning, you may want to give your property to a professional management firm in order to free your time for more profitable use. In choosing a management firm, talk to owners of similar property who are using professional management. This choice can be very important. I do not recommend signing a management contract unless you feel the management firm fully understands your goals and you have a feeling of trust in turning over your property to the firm.

ACQUIRING MANAGEMENT SKILLS

If you obtain professional management, your costs will range between 5 percent and 10 percent of the gross. One problem with professional management is that they have numerous properties to consider and many problems. You are only concerned with your own property. If you can acquire the management skills needed, you can do a far better management job on your own property than a management firm can possibly do. You can obtain these skills not only from experience but also from courses in property management given by a number of professional organizations.

The Institute of Real Estate Management (IREM) of the National Association of Realtors is a large national organization of professional property managers. They provide courses of training leading to the professional designations:

CPM—Certified Property Manager

RM—Accredited Resident Manager

While they offer excellent courses, an applicant for these designations must be a real estate licensee. For information on their program, contact:

Institute of Real Estate Management

of the National Association of Realtors

430 North Michigan Avenue

Chicago, IL 60611

The Real Estate Management Brokers Institute (REMBI) is an affiliate of the National Association of Real Estate Brokers, which is primarily an organization of black brokers. They offer the professional designations:

CRM—Certified Resident Manager

CREM—Certified Real Estate Manager

They offer courses of study particularly relevant to urban property. For information, contact:

National Association of Real Estate Brokers

1025 Vermont Avenue NW, Suite 1111

Washington, DC 20005

The National Apartment Association represents owners of apartment and multiple family units. As an owner, you can benefit from the courses they offer. They offer the professional designations:

CAM—Certified Apartment Manager

CAMT—Certified Apartment Maintenance Technician

For information, write:

National Apartment Association

1825 K Street NW, Suite 604

Washington, DC 20006

The Building Owners and Managers Institute International (BOMI) offers a

number of excellent courses for investors and managers. They also offer the
professional designation:

RPA—Real Property Administrator

For information write:

Building Owners and Managers Institute International
1221 Massachusetts Avenue NW
Washington, DC 20005

No state shall . . . deprive any person of life, liberty or property without due process of law.

—Constitution of the United States
Amendment XIV, July 28, 1868

15

Tenant Selection and Leases

Your tenant and the lease terms will materially affect the value of your property. Whether it is a rooming house or a shopping center, you want to obtain the best tenant possible. Quality tenants mean fewer management problems as well as lower expenses, which make the property more desirable to purchasers.

Credit reports, as discussed in Chapter 14, can eliminate many marginal or problem tenants before the property is rented. Generally a poor credit report and disregard for maintenance of your property go hand in hand.

PROBLEMS WITH COMMERCIAL TENANTS

A commercial tenant going through bankruptcy or corporate reorganization can mean uncollected and even uncollectible rent. If financial problems have arisen prior to the rental, then a credit report will indicate that the tenant is unable or unwilling to pay obligations on time. A vacant store is generally preferable to a problem tenant. Besides the financial loss from a problem tenant, you can expect an emotional loss in the form of stress. More important, having a problem tenant occupying premises under a lease will preclude you from making the premises available to a quality tenant.

BUSINESS FAILURE RATES

New businesses have extremely high failure rates. Two of the major reasons for failure of new businesses are undercapitalization and a lack of knowledge about running the particular business. You should be leary of prospective new tenants for a commercial location who do not have a proven success record making decisions in a similar business. Unfortunately, it is human nature to think the field is greener on the other side of the fence. People who know one business well and make money in it are nevertheless good candidates to lose money in a business they know little or nothing about. When you consider the fact that over 50 percent of new businesses fail within the first year and fewer than 25 percent are still in existence after three years, you can understand the problems relating to renting to new businesses.

Failing businesses can hurt your ability to rent to qualified tenants. Several business failures in succession at one location can give a location a bad reputation, discouraging other firms from moving in.

A mini-mall was completed in a resort city in a choice central location. The mall was exceptionally well designed with massive beams. There were five stores on each side of a wide, red brick promenade leading off the street. It had beautiful plantings, and I was sure it would be a winner. The owner, however, became over anxious to rent these small shops, which averaged about 500 square feet. He apparently rented to the first tenants who were willing to pay the rent. The initial tenants were:
1. A religious book store.
2. A "head shop" selling drug-related paraphernalia.
3. A coffee market carrying dozens of coffees blended to the customer's preference.
4. An electric razor repair shop owned by a retired gentleman who wanted to remain active.
5. A waterbed shop.
6. A mod clothes store.
7. A store specializing in African imports.
8. A small restaurant with outside tables.
9. A jewelry store.
10. An art gallery.

After only a few months the only original tenants remaining were the razor repair store and the religious bookstore. Since then, the mall has had a succession of tenants. The result has been a high vacancy factor, rent collection problems and lower rents than could be possible from successful tenants. While a horror case, it is not a solitary example of poor tenant selection.

GETTING SUCCESSFUL BUSINESSES

On my own commercial property and on property I formerly managed, I would actively seek out tenants. I looked for successful businesses within the area and analyzed what advantages my property had over their present locations. I would then contact the businesses. While often they were on leases, on two occasions businesses I contacted liked my proposal and decided to open up second locations.

Some of the important points which allowed me to get successful businesses and professional people to move included:

1. More space.
2. Better parking.
3. Better location for the type of business.
4. Lower rent, when a business did not require the quality location it had. For example, I talked a plumbing wholesaler into moving from a main street to a side street which offered better parking and about half the rent.

In a tenant search, I particularly look for businesses of the same general type as are already located close to my vacancy. Businesses like to be in an area where others in the same business are located. Several firms together attract more customers than if they were separate. Also, many businesses generate business for allied firms.

You should consider businesses such as franchises which are expanding geographically. If you feel a location is suitable for a franchise, call the executive offices and talk to someone in their real estate department. Follow up the call with a letter. Often franchises want desperately to expand. One limiting factor is the ability to obtain new sites. I have usually received a very positive reaction when I have contacted franchises.

NEGOTIATING ACCEPTABLE LEASES

After you have located a tenant, you must negotiate a lease acceptable to the tenant that also serves your best interests.

Month-to-month rentals should be avoided for commercial rentals unless you want to keep the property available for some reason, for instance, if you felt you could get a national tenant for a location but needed immediate income. This type of rental agreement can generally be terminated by either the tenant or the owner by giving one month's notice. In all fairness, I would not enter into such a rental without full disclosure to the tenant. Keep in mind that a tenant willing to take a short-term rental will generally be fairly shaky.

Even for residential property, a month-to-month tenancy is not desirable. Tenants who want such a rental usually do not expect to remain long. When tenants have short stays, it means greater expenses to the owner for advertising and related rental expenses, much greater maintenance and a higher vacancy factor. It is seldom that a property does not require some work between tenants or that new tenants are willing to pay rent from the day the premises are vacated.

Rental agreements should generally be for at least one year. As the desirability of a location increases, the length required for the lease can be increased. In inflationary periods we have experienced a change in attitudes of landlords toward leases. Many landlords are now unwilling to sign multiyear leases at fixed rents or even leases with fixed-step increases. They want either short leases, such as one year, or multiyear leases tied in with an inflationary index such as the Consumer Price Index.

INFLATIONARY CONSIDERATIONS

Some landlords have found that even leases tied into the Consumer Price Index have failed to protect them from inflation. No one expected fuel oil prices to rise from thirteen cents to a dollar a gallon in only a couple of years. Electrical rates in some areas have increased 200 percent in a short time. The fuel and utility prices have risen at a far faster rate than the various consumer indexes. These increases have turned a number of excellent investments into negative cash-flow situations despite the fact that they were tied to an index.

A *triple net lease*, which is normally just called a net lease, is a lease in which the tenant pays for all maintenance and repair expenses as well as taxes and insurance. The owner is guaranteed a net amount each month. A *double net lease* is a lease in which the tenant pays for all maintenance and repairs, but the lessor pays the taxes and insurance.

Net leases of both types are usually long term. Long-term net leases, in which the net amount to the owner is fixed, do not increase the owner's income from the property. In addition, during inflation the value of the net rental decreases every year. The solution is, of course, to tie the net rental into either the Consumer Price Index or one of the wholesale indexes. This would allow the lessor to retain the same relative purchasing power originally bargained for no matter what happens to the economy.

PERCENTAGE LEASING

If you have an exceptionally good location, you don't have to be satisfied with a set rent. It is possible to share in a tenant's success. This can be accomplished through a percentage lease. Under a percentage lease, the lessee pays the lessor an agreed percentage of his or her gross income. Generally, businesses having higher markups pay higher percentages of the gross. A percentage lease should also require a minimum rent, with inflation increases, as well as a covenant to remain in business. This protects the landlord against a tenant closing down and paying only the minimum rent. Because each business brings customers for other businesses, if one trade closes down it hurts the gross of other nearby businesses as well.

The percentage lease should also set forth the period of time the lessee has to begin operation. Otherwise the lessor could receive only the minimum rent for a protracted period of time.

Some percentage leases have *graduated percentages*. As the gross increases beyond a particular amount, the percentage decreases. This encourages a firm to advertise and have sales. The net effect of graduated percentages can be greater net income for the lessor. Many percentage leases contain *recapture clauses*. If a tenant fails to attain a particular gross, the lessor has the right to end the lease, thus protecting the lessor against a poor operator.

With percentage leases, you want your tenants to advertise. Leases in shopping centers frequently require the tenants to pay an additional percentage of their gross for cooperative advertising such as shopping-center-wide sales. Remember, you as the lessor want an increased gross, as this means higher rents.

Percentage leases in shopping centers usually set forth the hours stores must be open. If some stores would stay closed on a Sunday afternoon, for example, it would reduce the gross of the stores which are open. Percentage leases normally also prohibit the tenant from having a warehouse sale or other off-premise sale where the gross would not be subject to the rent percentage.

Lessors usually require tenants under percentage leases to use a specified type of cash register which keeps a running total and cannot be set back. Honesty in reporting is not usually a problem with larger tenants. There can be problems with some smaller stores. There are protection services that will check to see that all sales are properly run up on the registers.

Besides the minimum, percentage leases have built-in protection against inflation. As the costs of the goods increase, the gross increases without any real increase in sales.

OTHER LEASING PROVISIONS

Design Approval.   In some malls the leases require design approval, allowing for desired uniformity.

Assignment or Subletting.   Generally, commercial leases should have provisions against assignment or subletting. Then, if a tenant wishes to leave, you have an opportunity to renegotiate terms with a new tenant. In a lease assignment, the new tenant assumes the lease and pays rent directly to the owner. In a sublease the new tenant is the tenant of the old tenant, not of the owner. By allowing a tenant to sublet, the tenant can take advantage of inflation by getting a higher rent than he or she is paying. Of course, if you are the tenant, you want the right to sublet.

Use of Premises.   Commercial leases normally specify the use that must be made of the premises. You may want a restaurant in a location to help other rentals you have. You would not want the lessee to open a pornographic book store. Some uses can increase insurance costs.

Leasing Raw Land for Storage.   You should be wary of leasing raw land for storage or disposal of chemicals. A few months' rent has left some owners with worthless property. There have been several cases in which tenants have been in the business of disposing of toxic wastes. The tenants have stored tens of thousands of barrels of waste on a property, ostensibly temporarily, but have then walked away, leaving owners with a horrendous problem. Besides specifying use, you can protect yourself by a lease clause prohibiting the storage of toxic, explosive or otherwise hazardous materials.

Illegal Use of Premises.   All leases should have clauses which allow the landlord to terminate the lease if the premises are used for illegal purposes such as gambling or prostitution. Some leases today specifically prohibit X-rated movies, explicit sex books and other related activities which, while legal, have a negative effect on rentals and values in the area.

Televisions.   Today, television interference can be an important problem. Some leases prohibit use of powerful radio equipment. The installation and removal of antennas for radio or television can damage the roof. Many leases prohibit them. Often commercial and residential buildings have a master antenna for the tenants.

Noise.   Leases frequently have clauses about noise to protect against residential tenants playing loud music or commercial tenants using disturbing loudspeakers. Some leases actually specify decibel levels. Residential leases frequently have clauses on playing records and making other noise after a particular time.

Weight Restriction.   Second-floor commercial and residential leases often have weight restrictions. Overloading a building can damage the structure. Some older apartment buildings ban waterbeds both because of the weight and because damage can result if the bed ruptures.

Injuries on Premises.   Liability for injuries resulting from the condition of the premises is normally covered in commercial and residential leases. Many leases require the tenant to indemnify the landlord for any losses suffered because a third party is injured on the premises. Often commercial leases require tenants to carry liability insurance.

Number of Occupants. Residential leases customarily specify the number of occupants allowed. Lessors have an interest in this because a higher occupancy means higher utility costs and greater wear and tear on the premises.

Other Restrictions. Leases can also specify whether pets are allowed, whether children are allowed, hours for use of recreational facilities, etc.

Holdover Clauses. At times a tenant will stay after the end of a lease or after notice has been given to vacate. This can create a serious problem, especially if you have rented the premises to a new tenant. The problem can be solved with a holdover clause. What this clause does is to set a huge rental for a holdover. It forces a tenant to either renegotiate a lease prior to its expiration or to vacate as agreed. An example of a holdover clause would be a month-to-month rental at $4,000 per month if the tenant remains in possession after the $500-per-month lease expires. With an increase like this, you know the tenant will not hold over.

Fire. Leases customarily cover the rights and duties of the parties if the premises are totally or partially destroyed by fire. The lease may merely be suspended until the premises are rebuilt, or the landlord may have the option of notifying the tenant that the premises will or will not be rebuilt. If the tenant caused the fire, the lease could provide that the rent continue.

Electrical Service. Some tenants require greater electrical service than a building can provide. A commercial lease normally requires the tenant to pay for any additional electrical installation services required.

Right of Inspection. Leases should allow the lessor the right to enter the premises for inspection purposes, to make repairs and to show the premises to prospective buyers.

Options. If an option to purchase is given, it should be either for a very short period of time or tied to a Consumer Price Index so that you are not giving away the benefit of inflation.

Often leases provide options to renew for set periods. You should be certain they reflect economic changes. Right now $10,000 per month might sound great, but we don't know what this amount will be worth in ten years. Option prices should also be tied to economic indicators.

Even though a tenant is on a month-to-month rental, a lease is nevertheless important. A lease sets forth the rights and duties of the parties and will serve to prevent problems or disagreements.

You can purchase many types of lease forms from stationery stores. While they will save you money in attorney's fees, it might very well be the kind of savings you cannot afford. I recommend, except for simple residential leases, that you have a knowledgeable real estate attorney draft your leases. It is too important an area for a do-it-yourself project.

Give a man the secure possession of a bleak rock, and he will turn it into a garden; give him a nine-year lease of a garden and he will convert it into a desert. The magic of property turns sand into gold.

—Arthur Young, 1787

16

Selling Your Property

When should you sell real property? There are really only two times to sell. One is when you need money for personal use and you cannot obtain it without a sale. The second is when you believe another investment will better meet your needs.

REASONS FOR CHANGING PROPERTY

Some of the good reasons for changing property include:
1. The belief that another property offers greater appreciation potential.
2. The desire for a greater spendable income.
3. The desire for greater depreciation.
4. The desire to reduce management problems.
5. A desire to exchange a more speculative investment for a more secure one.
6. A belief that anticipated changes will lessen the desirability of the property.
7. The belief that a property can be sold at a price greater than the purchase price of similar property.

REAL ESTATE COUNSELORS

If you are undecided whether to sell, trade or continue to hold the property, I suggest you contact a real estate counselor. The fee for professional counseling is generally money very well spent. You will want a counselor with the professional designation of CRE, which designates a member of the American Society of Real Estate Counselors (ASREC) of the National Association of Realtors. Membership in the organization is limited to professionals with demonstrated knowledge and experience. To find a CRE, check Real Estate Counselors in the yellow pages of your local phone book. You can be sure if a counselor has achieved a CRE designation as it will appear in his or her advertisements. You can obtain a list of ASREC members by writing:

American Society of Real Estate Counselors of the
National Association of Realtors
430 North Michigan Avenue
Chicago, IL 60611

UNDERSTANDING ALL ASPECTS OF THE SALE

Taxes. Prior to accepting a purchase offer or placing your property on the market, you should fully understand the tax consequences of a sale. If you will have a large capital gains and expect to be investing the sale proceeds in another property, you don't really want a sale; you should be considering an exchange. Exchange techniques and advantages are covered in Chapter 11.

Value. Before putting your property on the market, you should first of all consider what it is worth. What you may have paid for it does not determine its value and may bear little relation to what it will sell for.

No appraiser can tell you exactly what a property will sell for. Appraisal is not that exact a science. However, an appraiser can usually predict the price range into which a sale will fall. For example, a lot may be worth between $45,000 and $55,000. An appraiser could determine this range by various means; most commonly he or she will analyze actual sale prices of similar property. By checking similar property available on the market, you can find asking prices. Property is usually listed for sale at the high edge of the sales range or above it. Therefore, the fact that property similar to yours is listed at $100,000 does not mean that either that property or your property will sell for $100,000.

Value is of course influenced by supply and demand. Demand is meaningless unless the demand is coupled with purchasing power. If there are more buyers than sellers, prices tend to rise while, conversely, a market with more sellers than buyers tends to reduce prices.

When a market has become limited, property may sell for far more than similar property in the past. As an example, the last available lot in a desirable subdivision could conceivably sell for far more than the price received at the last comparable sale.

When your checking has given you some general ideas of value, contact one or more competent real estate brokers who are active in your area. You may find that your facts are not accurate or up to date. A professional real estate agent will usually have accurate sales figures of comparable property.

DETERMINING LISTING PRICE WITH AN AGENT

If the real estate agent asks what you want for the property, do not give a figure. This can be very dangerous. If you quote a low price, some unethical agents will tell you that you really know the market and that is exactly what they think it is worth. Agents often forget that their first responsibility is to the owner and not to earning a commission. By taking a listing at a below-market price, such agents seek to enhance the likelihood of their selling the property and earning a commission. Often owners sell at huge profits only to later learn that they actually sold their property at a bargain price. Other agents will try to buy the listing by quoting an unrealistically high value. They are offering more than the other agents in order to appeal to your greed. After the agent gets the listing, he or she will then start coming up with good comparables and try to prepare the owner for a much lower price.

When an agent suggests a listing price, I ask why. I want the agent to defend the price suggested. If an agent cannot adequately support his or her recommendations, I am not interested in working any further with that agent. You want to work with a professional, not an amateur.

I have mentioned the extremes for your protection. Most real estate licensees are honest and knowledgeable. You will probably develop a relationship of trust and respect with one or two licensees. When such relationships develop, I recommend that you try to deal exclusively with those agents.

INDEPENDENT FEE APPRAISERS

If after your own investigation and the advice of real estate agents you are still not decided what price to ask, I strongly recommend that you hire an independent fee appraiser. The dollars you spend will be well worth it. Besides peace of mind, a professional appraisal can save you the time which could be wasted in trying to sell a property at an inflated price or the dollars you might lose if you sold the property at too low a price. (See Chapter 8, pp. 73–74, for recommendations about finding a professional appraiser.)

NEIGHBORS ARE LIKELY BUYERS

Before you give a listing on your property, I recommend that you contact your tenant(s) and adjoining property owners. These are the logical buyers for your property. Over the years I have sold several properties to tenants and I myself once purchased a house I had formerly rented. In addition I have sold lots, a commercial building and a farm to adjacent property owners. Many owners are like the old farmer who only wants what is his and what is next to his. A few minutes of work could conceivably save you thousands of dollars in commissions. While I don't begrudge paying a sales commission, there is no sense in paying one when a buyer is easily found.

OPEN LISTINGS

Some real estate agents will agree to work with an open listing. Under this type of listing the licensee earns a commission only if he or she actually sells the property. If the owner sells it or any other agent sells the property, then the agent with the open listing has not earned a commission. While an open listing might sound like a good deal to you since you can sell the property yourself without paying a commission, it is actually a very bad deal for the owner. Very few brokers will advertise an open listing, since it means he or she really doesn't control the product advertised. If a salesperson has the choice of trying to sell a property on an exclusive listing where a commission is assured or an open listing where the owner is trying to sell the property without paying a commission, you can guess which property will get the greatest sales effort.

EXCLUSIVE RIGHT-TO-SELL LISTINGS

I recommend that you give an exclusive right-to-sell listing to a broker whom you trust. Under an exclusive right-to-sell listing, the broker earns a commission if the property is sold during the listing by anyone, including you the owner. If you don't want to give an exclusive right-to-sell listing because you have already talked to several possible buyers, I still recommend the exclusive right-to-sell listing with an exclusion. Most brokers will agree to exclude several named buyers for a short period of time such as ten days. Now you will have a real club for the buyers. If they are at all serious, they have ten days to buy without obligating you to a commission. They will realize that they can make a more advantageous deal right away than they can expect to make after the ten-day period. The exclusion will often result in a quick sale.

If the named individuals don't buy, chances are they were lookers only and not serious buyers. People such as this can waste a great deal of your time.

MULTIPLE LISTING SERVICES

Generally, you should give a listing to a broker who belongs to a major multiple listing service so that the property will get maximum coverage. However, multiple listing services generally don't do much for specialty property such as farms, motels or industrial buildings. Giving these listings to large groups of salespeople who primarily sell residential property isn't really going to help you in finding a buyer. In fact, giving some specialized listings to multiple listing services could cause more harm than good. Good sales prospects can be lost by salespeople who lack the specialized knowledge and experience necessary to sell the property.

SMALL OR LARGE BROKER?

Some small real estate offices will not advertise a property adequately. For residential property you are usually better off giving a listing to a larger office. The large firms with many salespeople and offices, as well as franchise brokers, usually specialize in residential property. However, many small offices specialize in particular geographical areas where they may actually dominate the real estate market. In such cases the small office would be preferable. Smaller offices often specialize in other than residential property, so they might be best for nonresidential sales. As an example, I know of several smaller brokers who sell only industrial property and one small broker who sells only mobile home parks. These specialists can usually do a far better job for nonresidential property sales than general offices.

Some brokers just want to get listings. They give them to their multiple listing service and hope someone else can sell them. This type of broker won't do enough for you; you want a broker who will use his or her best efforts to obtain a buyer.

GO TO ESTABLISHED PROFESSIONALS

With the number of real estate licensees around, everyone seems to know people in the business. Many owners give listings out because of friendship rather than expertise. Don't mix business with friendship. It is bad business to give a listing to an office which is not active in the particular geographical area of your listing or in the particular type of property which you have for sale. In addition, real estate has attracted many retirees and parttime people. Because these people do not have to be successful in real estate, they usually are not. You want your listing handled by an office staffed with successful people who really want your property to sell and are willing to work to accomplish that sale.

WHY IT PAYS TO SELL THROUGH A BROKER

There are some good reasons for paying a commission to a broker rather than trying to sell your property on your own. To start with, when you advertise your own property, you will be spending a good deal of time talking to brokers who will be trying for the listing. Besides brokers, owner ads attract the jackals who are out to steal your property rather than pay a fair price. They will often try to trade near-worthless property for yours.

The most important reason for selling through an agent is qualified buyers. Consider how you purchased your real estate. Chances are you went to brokers because you realized that they would know what was available and could show you a number of properties. Other qualified buyers are no different from you. They seek the help of experts and don't want to waste their time running down individual owner ads.

Another important reason for selling through a broker is that it is often very difficult to handle negotiations with a buyer. Direct negotiations often become emotional. Many deals are lost because of the natural emotional reactions of the parties involved. I have purchased and sold property directly as well as through agents. In most cases I don't feel that selling directly actually saved me money.

A professional real estate agent realizes he or she represents you and not the buyer. A professional will not try to force an inadequate offer on you for acceptance. Unfortunately, some licensees are not professional and care more about their commission than your welfare. They may bring several salespeople and brokers to try to persuade you to accept an inadequate offer. Over the years several agents have tried these tactics with me. I will no longer have dealings with any of them and have told them why. On the other hand, a professional will actually advise you against accepting an inadequate offer and suggest possible counter offers when appropriate.

Real estate agents will usually try for as long a listing as possible. In most areas, exclusive listings for homes are for a three-month minimum. In resort areas they could be for longer periods. Vacant industrial or commercial property could be listed for one year or even longer. Generally, the more saleable a property is, the shorter the listing. Since a listing ties you to a broker for a set period of time, you should only sign with a broker you have confidence in.

LOWERING COMMISSIONS

I don't recommend trying to get a broker to take a listing at a commission lower than the customary rate charged for similar property in the area. While a broker may agree to a lower rate, the effect will be that salespeople will give the property a second-class treatment, showing it only when they have no other full-commission properties to show.

While I have had a real estate license for years, I don't try to get part of the commission back because of my license. When you cut someone's profit, you are also going to cut his or her effort. Money motivates.

PREPARING PROPERTY FOR SALE

Before you place your property on the market, you want to make sure it is ready to be shown. You want your property to present as favorable an image to a prospective buyer as possible. Many potential buyers are lost by owners who don't prepare their properties for sale.

IMPROVEMENTS FOR PROFIT

An owner I know wanted to sell a 2½-acre parcel that had an old farmhouse on it. An appraiser told the owner it should bring $40,000. The owner made the following improvements:

1. Paint, inside and out	$1,500
2. Kitchen remodeling	3,000
3. New carpeting and tile	2,000
4. New small horse barn	4,000
5. White wooden fencing and corral	2,700
6. Bass to stock small pond	200
7. Mallard ducks for pond	50
	$13,450

The owner sold the property for $69,500, or $29,500 more than it had been appraised at before the remodeling. Each dollar spent in preparing the property for sale actually resulted in over two dollars more in the sale price.

While every improvement will not improve the sale price, many will. You should consider possible improvements and how the improvements will affect the value. If an improvement cannot be expected to return at least 150 percent of the cost in added value, then I recommend the improvement not be undertaken. I know from experience that actual costs frequently exceed estimates.

IMPROVEMENTS INCREASE SALEABILITY

Besides increasing profit, improvements also increase saleability. A dirty property is difficult to sell; cleaning it up will increase its saleability. Paint and landscaping expenses usually improve saleability as well as increase value.

> A number of years ago I purchased a lakefront lot for $7,500. The lot, which had been on the market for a year, was so fully wooded it was not possible to see the lake from the road. In fact, because of brush and scrub trees, you couldn't even walk from the road to the water without getting badly scratched. I hired a young man with a chain saw to clear off the scrub trees, leaving only a dozen fine pine trees. It cost $350 to clear the lot and haul away the trash and trees. When I was finished, several excellent building sites were apparent. The pine trees looked majestic and the view from the road was excellent. Two weeks after I purchased the lot, I was offered $15,000 for it, even though I was not looking for a buyer. I turned the offer down because I wanted the lot for my own home, which I have since built.

Repainting.   When you repaint, colors are important. Don't try to copy the decorators with currently fashionable colors. Although people like to visit far-out models, they are usually more traditional in their own homes. You seldom go wrong with light interior colors such as white or cream. Light colors tend to make rooms appear larger and convey the impression of freshness. For exteriors, light colors accented with slightly darker complementary colors usually work very well.

Wallpapering, Paneling and Carpeting.   A little textured wallpaper, perhaps on one wall in a livingroom or as wainscotting in a dining area, can help a sale. If a wall needs plastering, it is usually less expensive to put up prefinished plywood paneling than to replaster. Carpets should be in medium-light colors such as beige.

Flowers, Plants and Trees.   Seeding and seasonal flowers can help a building. Blooming petunias or other flowers outside an apartment building, home or even a commercial building can do a great deal to attract a potential buyer. You can buy many plants and even young trees at discount houses and even supermarkets. If you need help in planning your plantings, consult a nursery. Many have reasonable planning services.

Lighting Fixtures.   For older residential units I have found that new lighting fixtures in the kitchen, dining area and bath are well worth the investment. For the bath I usually combine the lighting fixture with a large, modern, mirrored medicine cabinet. Remember that as a seller you are competing with other sellers. You want your property to be more desirable than competing properties.

Furniture. If a property is being sold furnished, you must avoid overfurnishing it. Too much furniture or furniture which is too large makes rooms look crowded and small. Upgrading the furniture will improve saleability. It is difficult to sell a unit furnished in Salvation Army modern and get the maximum market price.

When I formerly owned a number of furnished units, I would watch the want ads. Frequently, because of divorce, death or the high costs of moving, an entire household of furniture can be purchased very reasonably. To buy a household of furniture from an ad, I would bring cash and a truck. I started laying down twenty-dollar bills on the kitchen table, counting to myself (the owner was counting also). When I stopped, I would say that this was the amount I would give for all the furniture including appliances (this was my opening offer). Because it was cash and right there, my initial offer was often accepted. This is actually the way many used furniture dealers operate; in fact, a dealer showed me this technique.

Other Features. Cleanliness is of course important. The kitchen appliances and bath fixtures must shine. I actually use a wax for this purpose. A roach or a rodent will usually ruin an otherwise favorable impression. The property should be well lighted when you show it and airy as possible. Drapes should be open and lights on. If a building has air conditioning, in summer you should turn it on at least an hour before showing the building.

DETERMINING HOW YOU WISH TO SELL A PROPERTY

You should have fully considered how you wish to sell a property before it is placed on the market. If you want cash, you should ask yourself why. Many people ask for cash but really don't need cash. If you intend to invest the cash in a safe, interest-bearing account, you are probably better off leaving some of the purchase price in the real estate. You will probably get a higher interest return, and you will have the security of the property.

Price can be a function of terms. You can sell a property for more money with a low downpayment than you could for cash. In the same manner, a property with a large assumable loan at favorable terms can be sold at more money than if new financing were required. I have sold property with no downpayment in cases where the buyer had good credit, but I was able to get a premium price and interest terms.

RECEIVING AN OFFER

Should you receive a verbal offer to purchase property, ask that the offer be reduced to writing even though it may be unsatisfactory. Once a person actually gives a written offer, that person usually starts to think in terms of actually owning the property. While the person might have thought, up until the time of the written offer, that he or she would not exceed a certain price, a written offer often makes a potential buyer ripe for a counter offer. I know that I have reevaluated my position and have accepted counter offers at prices I originally would not consider paying.

COUNTER OFFERS

When you receive an offer, you should realize that your acceptance will form a binding contract. If you give a counter offer, you are rejecting the buyer's offer and are saying that you won't accept the offer as made, but that you will agree to sell at the price and terms stated in the counter offer. If the buyer is nervous, you are giving the buyer an opportunity to back out of the purchase. Many buyers get "buyer's remorse" and look for opportunities and reasons not to buy. Therefore, don't counter offer if the basic offer is acceptable. If you try to wring the last penny from a property, you could lose the entire deal.

When you refuse an offer or give a counter offer, you are competing with the buyer. You are really saying, "No! I will pay more for the property." Not accepting an offer indicates you feel the property is worth more to you than the offer provided. If, on the other hand, you wouldn't consider buying a similar property at the price and terms offered, then you should seriously consider accepting the offer.

I generally give a counter offer rather than an outright rejection. I try to make the counter offer appealing by giving in on one of the following areas:

1. Price
2. Downpayment
3. Interest rates
4. Other loan terms

People want to think they have driven a hard bargain. They want to obtain some advantage from the bargaining. It really helps a buyer's pride to have purchased property at better terms than were originally offered. I have seen deals fail because an owner wouldn't allow a buyer to save face by giving even a token concession.

USE AN ATTORNEY WHEN NECESSARY

If you receive an offer that you don't fully understand, see an attorney. Don't accept the buyer's or broker's explanation as to what the written offer means. While most people are straightforward, there are some who will try for an advantage any way they can get it.

An elderly woman I know had ten acres of land for sale. The buyer offered $100,000 which, while less than she had been asking, was a reasonable price. The buyer offered only $5,000 down on a land contract but agreed to pay the balance of the purchase price within three years. The buyer also agreed to a 10 percent interest rate which, at the time, was a very high rate of interest for land contracts. The deal really looked good, but there was a twister. The buyer wanted release clauses on 2½-acre parcels by paying $23,750 for each release. The 2½-acre parcels were laid out as shown:

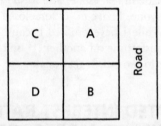

The owner sold the land at the price and terms indicated. Immediately after the land contract was signed, the buyer tendered $47,500 for the release of parcels A and B. The buyer made no further payments after receiving deeds to these parcels. The seller was left holding parcels C and D. Parcels A and B were the highway frontage parcels and were worth about $40,000 each. The two back parcels were worth only about $10,000 each. By setting up equal release amounts, rather than releases based on the parcels' relative values, the buyer was able to purchase $80,000 worth of real estate for a total of $52,500 ($5,000 down plus $47,500 to release parcels A and B).

I don't believe the buyer ever expected to pay for parcels C and D. I regard this particular buyer as a swindler.

DUE-ON-SALE CLAUSE

If you as a seller are going to carry back a mortgage or sell on land contract, you should consider a due-on-sale clause, which can mean early repayment of the loan should the property be sold. Even in states where the clause may not be legally enforceable, it can still be effective. If a buyer believes it is enforceable and pays off the loan at a sale, it is just as good as if it were fully enforceable.

ADVANTAGE OF BALLOON PAYMENTS

Chances are you don't want to leave your money in property for twenty years after you have sold it. If not, you should consider a balloon payment, which would require the buyer to pay you off in full at a particular time. For second mortgages five to seven years would be about average. Normally the buyer will have sufficient equity in the property, because of appreciation, that it can be refinanced. If the buyer cannot refinance the property when the balloon payment is due, you can either foreclose or rewrite the loan at more advantageous terms. The latter is the course I have taken in these cases. There is a lot of money to be made in real estate, and it isn't necessary to prosper by forcing foreclosure on anyone. I have never foreclosed a mortgage because of inability to refinance. While I have profited because of the misfortunes of others, I will not force misfortune on another. It isn't necessary to lose your human feelings in order to prosper in real estate.

GRADUATED INTEREST RATES AND PAYMENT MORTGAGES

I usually structure mortgages when I sell so that the buyer will want to pay me off early. I do this through a graduated interest rate and graduated payment mortgage. For the first one to two years I will usually agree to accept a below-market interest rate. For the third year the rate will rise to the market rate (at time of the sale). Each year thereafter the interest rate rises 1 percent. The buyer has a strong incentive to pay me off as soon as possible. In most states when the seller carries back the loan, the state usury rates don't apply. You should, however, check with a real estate attorney in your area prior to using this method.

LOANS STRUCTURED TO BUYER'S NEEDS

I have also structured loans with interest only for several years in cases where I have received a substantial downpayment. I have also sold property with payments actually less than the interest. In such a case, the amount due on the loan actually increases each month. Because of inflation in wages, a buyer can expect to be able to make a far greater payment in two or three years than he or she can now. Such loans allow young people to buy property. The increased earnings which come with experience, as well as inflationary factors, will allow these people to make payments easily in several years which might be impossible to make at the time of the sale.

In all your real estate dealings you will find honesty will help your profit, not hinder it. People whom I have treated fairly in past years have again done business with me. While I want profit like everyone else, the price is too great to pay if it has to be based on dishonesty or sharp dealings.

Mine is better than ours.

—*Benjamin Franklin*
Poor Richard's Almanac, 1756

17

What's For Me?

What others are investing in may not be the right property for you. Real estate investments should be tailored to each person's needs and abilities.

SHOULD YOU INVEST?

Before you rush out to buy up the world, you should first understand yourself. A property which upon a cursory analysis appears to be what you want, may not be suited at all for you. I recommend a self-analysis. Start by asking yourself the following questions:

1. Why am I interested in a real estate investment?_____
_____

2. How much time am I willing to devote to seeking out and managing real estate investments?_____

3. Am I willing to devote time at inconvenient hours to property or tenant requirements?_____

4. What types of maintenance and repair work am I capable of handling myself?_____
_____

5. Am I willing to get my hands dirty in maintenance and repair work?_____

6. How do I react to pressure situations and personal complaints?_____
_____
_____

7. What other property do I have that can be mortgaged or used for trade purposes?_____

_____

_____

8. How much capital am I willing to invest?_____

_____

9. Do I require a positive cash flow from my investment?_____

10. What would happen if I lost my entire investment?_____

11. How much actual negative cash flow am I able or willing to pay out each month?_____

12. What, if any, change in income do I expect over the next five years?_____

_____

13. How will this affect my ability to make payments?_____

_____

14. Am I willing to decrease my present standard of living for future benefits?_____
How much?_____

15. Do I like the excitement of a gamble or do I prefer greater safety?__

_____

16. Do I like the challenge of games like chess, which require organized plans, as well as changes in tactics to meet changed conditions?____

_____

17. Am I willing to make decisions which might adversely affect the lives of others?_____

18. Do I like working with people?_____

19. Is the nature of my investments, such as prestige, important to me?_

_____

20. My last year's federal tax return shows that my highest dollars of income were taxed at a rate of _____ percent.

21. My last year's state tax return shows that my highest dollars of income were taxed at a rate of _____ percent.

22. I expect my regular income to put me in the _____ percent bracket within five years.

COURAGE AND EMOTIONS AS INVESTMENT FACTORS

A young person with very few assets can often afford to be a high roller, risking all in a highly speculative investment. A person approaching retirement age who needs the capital for the coming retirement years is usually more interested in capital preservation coupled with a reasonable profit than making a killing. Risk capital, capital which will not affect a person's lifestyle can be invested in property offering a greater appreciation potential as well as a greater degree of risk.

I had an uncle, a high roller in his business and investments, who had a saying: "You lose your money and you have lost nothing, but you lose your courage and you have lost everything." While courage is required for every investment, the greater the downside risk, the more courage is required of the investor.

One of the smartest men I have ever known was wiped out financially in a building project. He had even borrowed on his cars, home and furniture in an attempt to save his investment, but all was lost. He never recovered from the loss, as he also lost his courage. This man took a salaried job and was unwilling to take any risks at all. He has no faith in his own judgment anymore and asks friends their opinions on any important decision he must make. No one can give him back his courage; it must come from within. For many people an investment in other than a savings account causes great emotional stress which they are unable to overcome.

To the other extreme, a large midwestern investor had been extremely successful. He owned over 800 fine residential units, lived on an estate with a gardener, maid and butler and had all of the trappings we customarily associate with great wealth. He invested in a building project and lost his shirt. The old adage, "People make money in businesses they understand and lose it in the other fellow's business," is all too often true. When I first met this investor, he was three million dollars in debt. Rather than go through bankruptcy, he went to his creditors and asked for their help. They agreed not to press him for the money, so he concentrated his efforts on recouping the losses. In California he rented a two-bedroom apartment and started using many of the techniques covered in this book, especially options. When I last saw the gentleman he had paid back almost one-third of the debt, was living in a beautiful home on a golf course and was driving a Mercedes. He never lost his courage and faith in his abilities.

RAW LAND AS AN INVESTMENT OPPORTUNITY FOR YOUNG INVESTORS

Raw land either in the form of developed lots or raw acreage is a negative cash-flow investment. Money must be paid out each month to make the mortgage payments as well as the taxes. To hold raw land, you must have sufficient disposable income to make the payments. While raw land can frequently be purchased and sold quickly at a profit, you should have the resources for a long-term holding period. Otherwise your failure to find a buyer could result in foreclosure, which would mean the loss of your downpayment as well as all other payments made.

Because land is a negative cash-flow investment, sellers are often willing to sell with very low downpayments. Therefore, raw land can be an excellent investment for young people with rising incomes but limited savings. As their income increases, they will derive more and more benefit from the investment because interest and taxes are deductible expenses for income tax purposes. When a person's income tax status rises to the 50 percent level (combined for federal and state income taxes), then each dollar in interest payments really costs only fifty cents. Uncle Sam is actually paying the other fifty cents for you.

A young person buying raw land might prefer buying larger tracts of land at lower prices. These larger parcels seldom fall in value but can appreciate enormously. One way to reduce the risk is to buy a number of these parcels in different locations.

RAW LAND AS A RETIREMENT HEDGE

Raw land also makes an excellent retirement hedge. Generally, people have their highest percentage of disposable income in the last 10 years of their working lives. Besides being at their earning peak, they have raised their families and have reduced family obligations and debts. Not only are they benefiting taxwise from the land investment, but appreciation will normally return their investment many times. In addition, the capital gains tax from a sale can be spread out over the retirement years when income is reduced.

People buying for retirement should be concerned with the quality of the land. They should buy smaller parcels of higher priced land within thirty miles of larger residential centers (in excess of one-half million people) or within five miles of cities in the 25,000 population category. Today I would recommend land purchases in the Sunbelt where we can expect the greatest population increases in the future. I recommend the parcel purchased be in the direction where greatest growth is forecast.

WHAT RAW LAND INVESTMENTS CAN DO

Raw land can offer alternatives. I know of a machinist who purchased forty acres about twenty miles outside a city where he lived. He paid $1,000 per acre for the parcel of marginal pasture land with large rocks and clumps of trees. He purchased the parcel with $4,000 down and monthly payments of $271.92 including interest at 7¾ percent. The man's idea was to retire at sixty-two (ten years after he purchased the parcel). He hoped to sell half the acreage then and have enough cash to pay off the other half, as well as cash for a downpayment to build a house.

It didn't work out the way the machinist had it planned. He was able to retire at fifty-eight and buy a Florida condominium. Six years after he purchased the property, he was able to sell his forty acres to a developer for $550,000. For his investment he had the pride of ownership of the land, a feeling of security the land gave him and more money from this one investment than he had totally earned in a working career of forty years.

OTHER PROPERTY TO CONSIDER

Not every land investment works this well, but it is seldom that property purchased at a reasonable market value fails to produce positive results. The difference between properties is primarily in the degree of profit.

LOTS

Some young people can't afford the downpayment or the payments on a house. They might, however, be able to purchase a lot. Lots can usually be purchased with low downpayments and at below-market interest rates.

Frequently, lot ownership can lead to home ownership. The lot with appreciation in value will often give the buyer sufficient equity to qualify for a loan to build a house or provide the trading material to trade for a house. In addition, a lot purchase allows the buyer to tie down the price of a major portion of the total house costs.

A lot can also provide psychic income in that it gives owners a sense of belonging to a community, of having roots. This feeling will motivate them in many ways which will lead to financial success.

COMMUTER FARMS

The small commuter farm should only be considered by a special person. Generally, purchasers must either bring their jobs with them to the property or be willing to commute an hour or more to and from work. The idyllic existence with a cow to give fresh milk loses some of its luster when you have to get up at 4:00 A.M. to milk the cow, feed a few animals and leave for work by 5:30 A.M. When you arrive home each night, the cow will need milking and there are evening chores. Weekends are not for ball games on the TV with a bottle of your favorite brew; they are devoted to working on fences, buildings and a thousand and one other things.

A small farm will probably also operate at a loss each year; if there is a profit, it will be only a few pennies for each hour of your labor. If you think you can hire someone to do the work for you, you had better be prepared to pay for it out of your pocket. Most smaller farms don't have sufficient income to support hired help. It is expensive being a gentleman farmer.

On the positive side, many people love commuter farming. With our increasingly impersonal, technical lifestyles, many people relish the manual labor and feeling of accomplishment that farms provide. The owners of small farms often live vicariously through their children, who are able to have pets, even horses. For many, the sacrifices of a small farm are worthwhile.

Also, a small farm can provide a great deal more than lifestyle. To start with, a farm has the advantages of depreciation of the improvements, equipment and even the cows. When a homeowner goes to the hardware store and buys a bucket of paint, it is not deductible, but when the small farmer buys the same paint, the government helps buy it since it is probably a deductible expense.

While few people go into a small farm for the profit motive, it usually works out as the best investment of their lives. Besides development possibilities there are thousands more city people seeking the same escape and willing to pay for it. We can expect this back-to-basics interest to continue well into the future, driving land prices higher and higher.

LARGER FARMS

Large farms today are really big investments. What were once considered just family farms are in many areas worth over a million dollars for agricultural use, not for development. Economical farm size varies depending upon the area and crops. For example, forty acres in avocados can be very profitable, but it might take several thousand acres in grazing land to make an equal profit in cattle.

The nation has lost a great deal of excellent farmland because of urban development. Generally, our cities are located on very choice farmland. In some areas, years of irrigation have resulted in the loss of farmland because of salt build-up in the soil. We have also seen some large corporations such as Tenneco and Purex buying up land for corporate farming.

While farm prices might seem high, they are nevertheless considerably lower than prices for European or much Asian farmland. We have had many foreign buyers for farmland, which has contributed to dramatic increases in value. We can expect these forces, as well as world population increases, to result in future farm value increases.

While large farms are frequently profitable, the profits tend to fluctuate. One year's profit can be followed by a huge loss. Real farming investments should only be made by people able to farm themselves or who have large disposable incomes to cover loss years. While there are many professional farm management firms providing complete service, they are expensive.

Large farms offer an investor pride of ownership, great depreciation on improvements (as well as on vineyards, orchards and livestock) and an excellent appreciation potential. To take full advantage of a large farm investment, you should be in the 50 percent tax bracket or higher.

DUPLEXES

The desire of many European immigrants was to own a duplex. They could live in one unit and collect enough rent from the other to make the payments and let them live for free. Today a duplex will not provide the income necessary to allow you to live for free, but they are nevertheless excellent investments. Since prices are determined more by demand than income, the demand for these units has led to prices far more than the rentals would justify. Even if both units were rented, in most areas of the country the rent won't make the payments.

Another problem is maintenance. While every homeowner has to make some repairs, owning a duplex or a rental house means you often have to do the same tasks for others. Also, many people today are unwilling to give up the privacy of a single-family home for a close neighbor. Living in close contact with another family can involve you with their personal lives. Many owners are unwilling to evict a tenant who has financial problems and fails to pay the rent. Others hesitate to raise rents even when their expenses have risen and the economy justifies a rent increase. If you are too much of a good guy who takes on the troubles of the world, you should not live in the same building as your tenants. You should either deal with your tenants on a strictly business basis or use professional management.

I once managed one unit of a duplex for a woman who lived in the other unit. She gave me the management of the unit when she

purchased the building. She did not want the tenant to know she was the owner and was therefore able to avoid the tenant problems of duplex ownership but retain the benefits of ownership. Besides income and appreciation, the owner of a duplex can depreciate the half of the building in which he or she is not living.

As residential units get larger, many problems actually decrease. Larger units can afford resident managers who can handle many problems. I know of one individual who has purchased many duplexes over the years. He gives one tenant in each duplex a rent deduction of twenty dollars a month in exchange for yard maintenance and minor repairs.

Professional management is available for every type of property. For residential properties the costs usually fall between 5 and 10 percent of the gross.

REALITIES TO FACE WHEN BUYING PROPERTY

The person who wishes to buy a house, fix it up and then sell it must be willing to live a nomadic existence and have a spouse willing to go along with it. Moving can be hard on children, who must change schools and friends. Ideally, these ventures are best for individuals or couples without children. It is hard for many people, after they have fixed up a place, to start all over again and take a drop in their standard of living while they are camping in another fixer-upper performing more renovations. Building or renovating is not an easy life. You must be willing to sacrifice present free time and pleasures for future benefits.

Commercial and industrial property can be excellent investments. If property is already well leased, the price and downpayment required will probably be substantial. Nevertheless, the demand for these investments is great. You can expect rentals to increase with inflation which, in turn, will increase the value.

Commercial or industrial property which is vacant or has problem tenants can frequently be purchased with little money down and at attractive prices and terms. These properties can be excellent investments for hardworking and imaginative people who have faith in themselves. If these people are able to obtain good leases, they will immediately obtain a substantial increase in their net worth. If they panic, they could end up accepting another marginal or problem tenant who does nothing for the property value. One problem is that these properties will have substantial negative cash flows until they can be leased.

I hope by now I have been able to provide you with enough information to give you some ideas as to the types of properties in which you wish to invest.

LONG RANGE GOALS TO THINK ABOUT

The next step is to ask yourself these two questions:

1. Where do I want to be financially in five years?_____

    _____

2. Where do I want to be financially in ten years?_____

    _____

With these goals in mind you are now ready for an investment plan to fulfill your needs and desires. If you are unable to formulate a plan, it is probably because your goal is not realistic. You must determine how much you are willing to sacrifice to achieve your goal.

Some people have very detailed plans as to the type of property to be purchased and even location. I know one person whose goals are to buy at least six options to purchase property each year. Mine are much simpler. They are as follows:

1. I will devote a minimum of eight hours each week to checking on investment opportunities.
2. I will buy a minimum of one parcel each year.

These two very simple steps have provided me with financial security.

Each Sunday I review what I have accomplished in the past week. My eight hours are spent checking brokers, properties and sometimes just general areas. I currently own property in three states. By requiring that I make at least one purchase each year, my plan stops me from constantly trying for the brass ring. The fantastic deals seldom come along. In the fall and early winter I really get busy if I haven't made a purchase. I must usually settle for a reasonable purchase at market value rather than a steal. I understand myself and know how much I like a bargain, but if I waited for the sure bargain, I would find myself lamenting, *I could have*. Also, by waiting for that terrific deal you allow prices to increase. The market price of nine months ago could be the dream price of today.

A plan such as mine will force you to make decisions. You are not a real estate investor until you make a purchase. Profits can't start until you do.

Appendix: An Investment Glossary

abstract—a property history including a copy of every recorded document dealing with a property. It is customarily examined by an attorney to determine whether an owner has a marketable title.

abstractive method—an appraisal method to determine land value. The value of improvements is deducted from the current sale prices of comparative property to determine the value of the land.

acceleration clause—a provision in a note which makes all payments due upon something happening. A due-on-sale clause is a type of acceleration clause making all payments due if a property is sold.

access right—right of ingress or egress of an owner.

accommodation party—a cosigner who agrees to be liable on a note. The credit of the accommodation party gives strength to the note.

accrued depreciation—the actual depreciation that has occurred on a property.

acre—43,560 square feet. A square acre would be approximately 208.7 feet by 208.7 feet. Four to five average city lots can be made from one acre.

advance fee—a fee paid in advance, usually to list a property for sale.

adverse possession—customarily known as "squatters' rights." A hostile user can acquire title after a statutory period of time. It usually requires payment of taxes.

age-life tables—appraiser's tables showing average economic life for various types of structures.

air rights—the right of a property owner to reasonable use of airspace over the property.

amortization table—a table showing the amount of the monthly payment necessary to fully liquidate a loan in a given period at a given interest rate.

amortized loan—a loan which will be fully paid by equal installments.

anchor tenant—a major tenant usually at one end of a shopping center. Other tenants benefit by the traffic between anchor tenants.

appraisal—an opinion of the current value of a property.

appreciation—an increase in value.

arbitrage—the taking advantage of interest rates by buying at one rate and selling at a higher rate by the use of a land contract or an all-inclusive loan.

as is—a phrase usually used to show that the seller is not warranting the condition of the property. It does not protect the seller in cases of concealment of defects or fraud.

assemblage—the process of bringing contiguous properties together under one ownership.

assessed value—the value placed by a tax assessor, usually below actual market value.

assessment—the amount actually assessed against a property for taxes or public improvements.

assets—property owned by or owed to a business or individual.

assignment—the complete transfer of all interests from an assignor to an assignee.

assumption—assuming and agreeing to pay a duty or obligation.

attractive nuisance—a condition existing on a property which could be expected to attract children and present a danger to them. In the case of an

attractive nuisance the owner may be liable for injuries suffered by a child even though the child may be a trespasser.

axial growth—growth of a city along the major traffic arteries leading from the community. The growth resembles the spokes of a wheel.

bailment—giving possession of personal property but keeping title. A bailment agreement could be used when borrowing on personal property if the lender holds possession for security reasons.

balance sheet—a financial statement showing net worth by listing assets and liabilities. Lenders frequently require balance sheets from loan applicants.

balloon payment—a final payment of a loan which is larger than the previous payments. While the payments might be based on a loan amortization, if the loan must be paid in full by an earlier date a final balloon payment is necessary.

Baltimore method—a means to estimate the value of a commercial corner lot. The corner lot is considered to be worth the sum value of a lot on each of the streets it faces.

band of investment method—a procedure to determine the capitalization rate that is the desired rate of return. The method should be used to appraise a particular income property. Using the income approach to valuation, the capitalization rate is divided into the annual net income to determine value.

banker's interest—interest based on a thirty-day month and a 360-day year.

beneficiary—the lender under a deed of trust.

blanket mortgage—a mortgage covering more than one property.

blockbusting—illegal procedure to induce panic selling based on fear of minorities entering an area.

boot—an additional sum of money or unlike property used to even out a trade. Boot is taxable as capital gains.

bracketing—determining a value by finding out sale prices of comparable properties having greater or lesser amenities. This technique is used in the market comparison appraisal method.

broker's net income—an optimistic income figure that does not consider a vacancy factor or management costs.

budget mortgage—a mortgage in which the borrower pays one-twelfth of the estimated taxes and insurance costs with each monthly payment so that funds will be available to pay them when they are due.

build-up method—a process to determine the capitalization rate by rating a risk-free and management-free investment and then adding for risk and management factors.

buyer's market—an economic situation in which there are few buyers and many sellers. Prices tend to fall during a buyer's market.

capital gain—a gain on the sale of real property or a business or investment asset when the asset has been owned for over one year. Capital gains are taxed at a lower rate than other kinds of income.

capital loss—loss from the sale of real property or other business or investment assets. A capital loss can be used to offset a capital gain in the year of the loss.

capitalization method—appraisal method whereby the net income of a property is divided by a desired rate of return for that property (capitalization rate) to determine value.

capitalization rate—the desired rate of return for a property. The greater the risk, the higher the rate.

cash flow—also known as net spendable, the cash which is left over after all cash outlays.

cash throw-off—net spendable, same as *cash flow*.

CC&Rs (covenants, conditions and restrictions)—private restrictions placed on the use of a property by owners.

certificate of eligibility—required of a veteran for a Veterans Administration (VA) loan.

certificate of occupancy—required by local government prior to occupancy of a new structure.

certificate of title—an abstractor's opinion as to the marketable condition of a title.

co-insurance—a policy requirement that a structure carry a minimum amount of insurance coverage in order for the insured to be covered completely for a loss. If the insured carries only a percentage of the coverage required, then the insured gets only that percentage of any loss, should there be a loss.

collateral—property given as security for a loan.

commercial acre—the original gross size of a parcel without deducting for losses for streets. While a property could be 160 commercial acres, the developable land could be only 120 acres.

comparables—property similar to an appraised property. Used for the market comparison method of appraisal.

component depreciation—the depreciation of the separate elements of a property based on each separate economic life. For example, a roof may be depreciated for fifteen years but the plumbing over twenty-five years.

compound interest—interest upon interest. The ordinary real estate loan is simple interest, not compound interest, since interest is paid each month as it accrues. If a payment were missed, then there would be compound interest.

concentric circle growth—growth pattern of a city in all directions from the core area.

condemnation—see *eminent domain.*

conditional loan commitment—a promise to loan on a property even though a buyer has not been located. The promise is conditioned on the buyer qualifying for the loan.

conditional sales contract—a sales agreement for personal property whereby the seller retains title but the buyer has possession. It is very similar to a land contract for real property.

condominium—a subdivision in which there is individual ownership of a unit of airspace but common ownership of the common areas with the other owners.

conventional loan—a loan made by a conventional lender without government insurance or guarantees.

corner influence—increased value for a corner parcel because of traffic and exposure on two streets.

cost approach—appraisal method whereby a value is based on the cost to replace a structure, less the accrued depreciation on the structure, plus the value of the land.

cubage—number of cubic feet in a structure.

curable depreciation—depreciation which can economically be cured.

curtail schedule—a loan schedule indicating how much of each payment is credited to interest and principal.

deadload—the weight of a structure itself. Liveload is the weight the floors can hold.

dealer—a person who buys and sells or develops property as a regular part of his or her income. Dealers are not allowed to take long-term capital gains on their profits, which are taxed as ordinary income.

declaration of restrictions—a declaration recorded by a subdivider of all covenants, conditions and restrictions. They are then usually incorporated into each deed by referencing the recorded restrictions.

declining balance depreciation—accelerated method of depreciation used for tax purposes. A fixed percentage is depreciated each year of a declining balance.

dedication—a gift of land to a public body. It is frequently required that a subdivider dedicate land for streets, etc., prior to subdivision approval.

deed—transfer document for real estate. It passes title from a grantor to a grantee.

deed in lieu of foreclosure—To avoid foreclosure, the buyer deeds the property to the lien holder. This procedure can create a problem. While foreclosure would have wiped out junior encumbrances, the lienholder by taking a deed now owns the property with the junior encumbrances against it.

deed of reconveyance—in cases of a trust deed, the deed given by the trustee to the trustor when the beneficiary has been fully paid. It returns the title to the trustor.

deferred maintenance—neglected maintenance of a property that would be required to return the property up to a desired condition.

deficiency judgment—a judgment obtained by a foreclosing lienholder when the proceeds of the sale are insufficient to pay off the lien. They are difficult to obtain and in some states they are not possible.

demise—the transfer of a leasehold interest.

demographic study—a study of the economic and social makeup of a population area, frequently required as part of a feasibility study.

deposit receipt—a purchase agreement or offer to purchase.

depreciation—the loss in value of property for any reason. For tax purposes, depreciation is treated as an expense.

depth table—appraiser's table showing the increased value of a parcel as it gets deeper. The back portion of a commercial lot is worth less than the front portion.

directional growth—development of an area primarily in one direction.

discount loan—a loan in which the interest is taken out in advance.

discounting a loan—selling an existing loan for less than its face value.

disintermediation—sudden withdrawal of savings from lenders. It results in a tight money market and occurs when greater interest rates are available elsewhere.

double escrow—the use of one escrow to both buy and sell a property.

down-zoning—the change in zoning to a more restrictive use.

earnest money—a deposit made by an offeror with an offer to show his or her serious intent.

easement—a right of ingress and egress over the land of another.

economic life—the period of time during which real property improvements contribute to the income of a property.

economic obsolescence—a decline in value due to forces outside a property itself such as a neighborhood change.

effective age—the age placed on a property by an appraiser using the replacement cost approach to value. It is based on the condition of the property and can be greater or less than chronological age.

effective gross income—the gross income less a vacancy allowance as well as an allowance for bad debts.

elevation—a builder's drawing showing views of a structure from the different sides.

eminent domain—the process whereby a government body can take private property for public use. The owner receives fair market value at the time property is taken.

encroachment—a trespass by the placing of an improvement on or over the property of another.

encumbrance—anything which affects title or use, such as a lien or an easement.

environmental impact report—report required for projects which will have a significant effect on the environment.

equity—the difference between the market value of a property and the liens against it. It is the owner's interest in the property.

escalator clause—a clause in a lease allowing payments to rise or fall.

escape clause—a clause which lets a party out of a lease or contract under specified conditions.

escrow—the neutral depository representing buyers and sellers in a transaction. The escrow managers handle the mechanics of real estate closings. In some states, closing of real estate transactions are handled by brokers or attorneys rather than escrows.

estate for years—a lease for a definite period of time. It does not automatically renew itself.

exclusionary clause—a deed clause excluding part of the property from the grant.

exclusive agency listing—a listing in which a broker is the owner's exclusive agent and is entitled to a commission if the agent or any other party sells the property: however, the owner can sell without an agent and pay no commission.

exclusive right-to-sell listing—a listing whereby the broker is entitled to a commission no matter who sells the property.

exculpatory clause—a clause in a lease that excuses the lessor from liability should the lessee be injured because of the condition of the premises.

extended coverage policy—extends the basic fire insurance policy to cover additional hazards.

extension of a lease—the continuation under an old lease as opposed to a lease renewal (new lease).

feasibility study—an economic study made to determine whether a proposed use is practical.

federal reserve system—the federal agency which regulates the money supply, interest rates and reserve requirements of member banks.

fee simple—the highest degree of ownership possible.

filtering down—the principle that housing tends to pass down to lower and lower economic groups.

financing statement—the notice filed by a lender for a personal property loan. It gives notice of the lien.

firm commitment—a loan commitment made for a particular property and a designated borrower, as opposed to a conditional commitment.

fixed expenses—expenses such as taxes and insurance that are fixed rather than variable.

fixture—an item, formerly personal property, that has been so affixed to real property as to be considered real property.

flat—residential unit all on one floor.

flat lease—a level payment lease where the rental remains unchanged for the lease period.

floor space—interior square footage.

foreclosure—procedure whereby unpaid lienholder sells the property to satisfy the lien.

free lot scheme—a lottery in which everyone wins, but there is a charge for transfer of the property which is actually the purchase price.

front foot—a measurement for some commercial property as well as waterfront property.

functional obsolescence—built-in obsolescence by design and construction.

gap loan—a temporary loan, usually at high-interest, obtained by a borrower who intends to obtain better financing.

governmental loan—a loan made by a lender with a government guarantee or insurance.

graduated lease—a lease providing for rent increases based on time or changing circumstances.

graduated payment mortgage—a loan in which payments are lower at first and increase as time goes on. It makes it easier for young people to purchase property.

grant deed—a deed used in some states, usually in conjunction with title insurance. The grantor warrants that he or she has not previously conveyed the property and that there is nothing detrimental the grantor knows of that has not been disclosed to the grantee.

granting clause—clause in a deed conveying title.

gross income—total income before any deductions.

gross multiplier—an appraisal method to get an approximate value. Gross income is multiplied times the multiplier number to determine value. (The multiplier varies by type of investment. The number is the number of times the gross that investors are paying for that type of property.) This method does not take into account unusual expenses.

ground lease—the lease of land without the improvements.

ground rent—that portion of the rent which is attributable to the land alone.

hard money loan—a loan where a lender actually puts up cash.

head lease—a master lease whereby the lessee subleases portions of the premises.

hold harmless clause—a clause in a lease whereby the lessee agrees to hold the lessor harmless for any loss suffered by the lessor because of the lessee's tenancy (example, the injury of a third party on the premises).

holdover clause—a clause in a lease providing for significantly higher rent should the tenant fail to vacate the premises at the end of the lease.

illiquid assets—assets not readily convertible to cash such as land.

impound account—a reserve for taxes and insurance kept by the lender. The borrower pays one-twelfth of the estimated taxes and insurance with each monthly payment.

incurable depreciation—depreciation for which the cost of correction is prohibitive.

index lease—a lease in which increases are tied to an index such as the Consumer Price Index.

index method—a method to determine replacement cost by taking the original cost to build and applying the increase in the construction cost index since actual construction.

internal rate of return—the present value of projected income expressed as an annual rate.

inverse condemnation—an action by an owner to force a government unit to take the property when the use has been materially restricted by wrongful government action.

jerrybuilt—cheaply constructed.

joint tenancy—an undivided interest shared by more than one tenant with the right of survivorship. Upon death of a joint tenant, his or her interests immediately go to the surviving joint tenants.

joint venture—a partnership for a particular undertaking.

junior lien—a subordinate lien. The priority of liens is determined by time of recording.

land contract—a financing arrangement whereby the seller finances the buyer. The seller keeps legal title and the buyer is given possession. The buyer does not get a deed until the property is paid for.

lease—a tenancy agreement.

leasehold interest—the interests of a tenant under a lease.

leverage—use of other people's money to make money, for example, by purchasing property with a low downpayment.

life estate—a life interest which cannot be willed or encumbered beyond the life of the life tenant.

like for like—a trade of property held for business or investment purposes. It allows a tax-free exchange.

limited partner—an inactive partner who contributes money only and whose liability does not extend beyond his or her investment.

liquidated damages—damages agreed on in advance in the event a contract is breached. Purchase agreements often call for the forfeiture of the earnest money deposit as liquidated damages should the buyer default.

listing—the agency agreement whereby a broker agrees to attempt to find a buyer, and the owner agrees to pay a commission should the broker be successful.

livable floor space—interior space measurement of each room, excluding interior walls and closets.

liveload—the weight a floor can carry in addition to its own weight. Very important in commercial and industrial properties.

loan-to-value ratio—the percentage of value that will be loaned on a property.

lock-in clause—a clause which, while allowing prepayment, requires that interest be paid as if the loan had gone to maturity.

margin of security—the lender's security, which is the difference between the mortgage and the property value.

market comparison approach—appraisal method whereby value is determined by recent sales prices of similar property.

market price—price actually paid.

market value—the price a willing buyer would pay to a willing seller.

marketable title—a title clear of objectionable liens and encumbrances and therefore acceptable to a buyer.

mortgage—a security device for real estate. In states following lien theory, the mortgagor retains title and gives the mortgagee a lien. In title-theory states, the mortgagor retains possession but gives the mortgagee the title as security.

mortgage guarantee insurance—private mortgage insurance (PMI) guaranteeing the lender against loss by buyer's default.

mortgage loan correspondent—individual or firm that arranges the sale of existing mortgages in the secondary mortgage market.

mortgage note—the note reflecting the mortgage debt. The mortgage is security for the note.

mortgage warehousing—interim financing whereby lender or loan correspondent borrows on an inventory of mortgages.

mortgagee—the lender or the seller of a property who receives the mortgage.

mortgagor—the owner or buyer of a property who gives the mortgage.

multiple listing—a listing supplied to a group of brokers.

narrative report—a comprehensive and complete appraisal.

negative cash flow—an investment situation in which the income is not sufficient to make the necessary cash outlays.

net listing—a listing where the broker receives as commission everything over a net sales price.

net-net lease—lease by which tenant pays all expenses except taxes and insurance.

net-net-net lease—lease by which tenant pays all expenses including taxes and insurance, also called a *triple net lease* or simply a *net lease*.

net profit—profit after all expenses.

net spendable—same as *cash flow*. Actual cash left from income after all cash expenses.

net worth—the total difference between a person's assets and liabilities.

noninstitutional lender—lenders other than banks, savings and loan institutions and insurance companies. Examples would be pension funds and private lenders.

obligatory advance—loan advances made under a construction loan by a lender as work progresses.

observed condition method—determining the effective age of a structure by its condition.

obsolescence—the loss in value of a structure because of design (functional obsolescence) or forces outside the property itself (economic obsolescence).

one hundred percent location—an idiom for the best commercial location in a community.

open-end loan—a loan which can be increased up to an agreed-upon limit.

open listing—a nonexclusive right to sell. The broker earns a commission only if he or she is successful.

option—a right given by an optionor to an optionee whereby the optionee can buy or lease the property of the optionor. To be valid, the optionee must have actually given consideration to the optionor.

optionee—the party who has the right to exercise an option.

optionor—the owner who has given an option.

orientation—the placement of a building on a lot with special regard for view or other environmental factors. For example, a builder might place a house on a lot so that the morning sun lights up the kitchen.

origination fee—a fee paid to a lender by a borrower for the privilege of obtaining the loan.

overimprovement—an improvement costing more than the income or increase in value will justify.

packaged loan—a loan that covers personal property as well as real property, such as a loan covering a motel building as well as the furniture.

paper—promissory notes given by the purchaser to sellers or lenders to finance a purchase. The term is generally used to include mortgages, trust deeds and notes.

participation loan—a loan agreement in which the lender takes an equity position (usually as a limited partner) in addition to the loan interest.

partnership—two or more people engaged in an enterprise as joint owners. Each is liable for any losses incurred. The courts will infer a partnership if there is an agreement to share profits.

party wall—a common wall on a property line maintained by both owners.

payback period—the period of time it will take for the income from an investment to return the downpayment to the investor.

percentage lease—a lease in which rent is a percentage of gross income.

percolation—the ability of soil to absorb water, important for septic systems.

periodic tenancy—a tenancy from period to period, automatically renewing itself unless a notice is given. An example is a month-to-month lease.

personal property—property other than real property, usually regarded as movable.

phantom income—the amount a payment reduces the principal on a loan. The income is not realized until the property is sold.

physical deterioration—depreciation caused by age and the wear and tear of use.

pitch—the slope of a roof. Generally, the greater the pitch, the longer the life of the roof.

planned unit development—a subdivision with an area owned in common.

pledge—the giving possession of personal property as security for a loan.

plot—a map of a subdivision showing individual lots and streets.

plot plan—the map of a lot showing the placement of a structure.

plottage increment—the increase in value when a number of small parcels are brought together to form a larger parcel.

points—a fee charged by a lender to give a loan. The points make up for a below-market interest rate. Each point is 1 percent of the loan amount. Lenders consider eight points paid in advance to be equivalent to an additional 1 percent in the interest rate.

prepayment penalty—a penalty charged by a lender for paying a loan in advance.

prescription—obtaining an easement over property by open, notorious and hostile use for a period of time prescribed by statute.

primary financing—first mortgages.

primary mortgage market—the actual granting of a loan directly by the lender to the borrower.

principle of change—the idea that values do not remain constant.

principle of competition—When extraordinary profits are being made in an area of investment, competition will enter the market and profits will drop.

principle of conformity—A property will achieve its maximum value in a homogeneous area of like property.

principle of dependency—The value of a parcel will be affected by changes in the use of surrounding property.

principle of diminishing returns—As demand is met, new units will result in reduced profit.

principle of integration and disintegration—Property goes through three stages: integration, equilibrium and disintegration (growth, stability and decline).

principle of substitution—A buyer will not pay more for a property than the price of a property having equal desirability.

principle of supply and demand—An increase in supply without an increase in demand will lower prices, while an increase in demand without a supply increase will raise prices.

profit and loss statement—operational statement showing income and expenses during a period of time.

pro-forma statement—an estimate of operating costs and revenue based on anticipated returns and expenses. It is used when there is no actual experience or when use is to be changed.

progression—an increase in value because a property is in a neighborhood of more expensive property.

progressive tax—income tax whereby tax rates increase as income increases.

prorate—to apportion costs at closing based on benefits received or to be received.

psychic income—the value of the feeling of pride in ownership.

puffing—a statement of opinion made by a seller. It is not a warranty.

purchase money mortgage—the mortgage given by the seller to finance the buyer.

purchase saleback or **purchase leaseback**—sale of real property by an owner to obtain capital with either a lease or purchase agreement from the lender.

quantity survey—a method of determining replacement cost in which each element of construction is separately priced.

quitclaim deed—a deed giving all interests a person has in a property. If the grantor has good title, good title is conveyed; if the grantor does not have good title, then good title is not conveyed.

racial steering—an illegal practice of directing minorities to a particular area.

real estate investment trust (REIT)—unincorporated group of 100 or more investors with limited liability under federal law. The investment trust is taxed on retained earnings only.

real property—land and that which goes with the land.

recapture rate—the rate at which invested principal is returned.

recording—filing a document for public record. Recording gives the public notice of an interest or transfer.

redlining—practice of lenders of refusing to lend within designated (redlined) areas. This practice is illegal in some states.

reformation—a court action to correct a mistake in a deed.

regression—a loss in value when a property is in an area of properties of lesser value.

rehabilitation—repairing a property without design change.

release clause—a clause in a blanket mortgage allowing a property to be released from the mortgage upon the payment of a stated amount.

remainder depreciation—the depreciation an owner has yet to take.

remodeling—the changing of a structure (interior or exterior).

renewal of a lease—replacing an old lease with a new one. (An *extension* continues an old lease.)

replacement cost—cost to build a substitute structure having the same utility value.

restoration—returning a structure to its original condition.

reverse mortgage—a mortgage whereby the mortgagor receives a monthly amount like an annuity from the mortgagee. The loan is not repaid until the mortgagor's death or until the property is sold.

rezoning—an actual change in the zoning.

right of first refusal—a right often given to a tenant to be allowed to meet any sales price and terms should the owner decide to sell.

rollover mortgage—a short-term mortgage amortized over a long period but due in only a few years. When due, it is rewritten at the then current interest rate.

salvage value—estimated scrap value of an improvement after it has exceeded its economic life. The salvage value is deducted from the cost of the structure prior to depreciating it, so when fully depreciated, the salvage value will be left.

SAM (sharing appreciation mortgage)—mortgage in which the mortgagee reduces the interest rate for an agreement to share in the profit when the property is sold.

satisfaction of mortgage—statement given by the mortgagee to the mortgagor when the mortgage has been paid in full. When the statement is recorded, the lien is removed.

Schwabe's law—principle that lower-income groups tend to pay a greater percentage of their income for housing than do higher-income groups.

seasoned loan—a loan with a payment history. A seasoned loan is desirable on the secondary mortgage market.

secondary financing—junior or second mortgages.

secondary mortgage market—the buying and selling of existing loans.

section—a parcel of land one mile square containing 640 acres.

security interest—a lender's interest in property which secures a loan.

seller's market—a market where there are few sellers and many buyers. Prices tend to rise in such a market.

setback—the distance a structure must be placed from a property line.

sinking fund—a fund whereby an amount is set aside each year so that the sum plus the interest it earns will be sufficient to replace an asset.

sky lease—lease of airspace.

special assessment—a tax assessment for improvements such as streets or sewers.

split-rate interest—a loan in which one interest rate is charged for the land and another rate for the improvements.

spot zoning—small areas of zoning change which do not fit the general use in the area.

square footage—exterior dimensions of a structure. A garage is excluded.

stagflation—a period of time when the economy shows inflation but no economic growth.

step lease—a lease with graduated increases. See *graduated lease*.

stock cooperative—a cooperative in which each owner owns stock in the corporation and has the right to occupy one unit.

straight line depreciation—a method of depreciation in which an equal amount is deducted each year as depreciation over the life of the asset.

straight loan—a loan in which interest only is paid and the entire principal must be repaid on the due date.

straw man—a purchaser used to conceal the identity of a purchaser or to hold title for some purpose other than actual ownership.

subdivision—a land division in accordance with state subdivision laws.

subject to mortgage—buying real estate without agreeing to pay the existing mortgage. When a buyer takes subject to a mortgage, he or she is not personally liable, but must make the payments if he or she wishes to retain the property.

subjective value—the use value of a property to the owner.

sublease—a lease between an original lessee (sublessor) and a sublessee. The sublessee is the tenant of the sublessor and not of the owner (original lessor).

subordination—an agreement in which an owner agrees that his or her lien shall be secondary to another mortgage that is to be given.

sum-of-the-years depreciation—an accelerated method of depreciation used for tax purposes for new residential structures.

surrender—the agreement between a lessor and lessee whereby the lessee returns possession of the premises to the lessor and the obligations of the parties are terminated.

sweat equity—equity in a property based on owner's actual labor on the property.

swing loan—a short-term loan usually made when a borrower has purchased a new home but has not yet sold his or her old home.

syndicate—usually a limited partnership (limited liability) made for investment purposes.

take-out loan—the permanent financing which replaces the construction loan.

tax shelter—a means of sheltering regular income from income taxes through depreciation.

tenancy at sufferance—a tenant holding over at the end of a lease without permission. The tenant is generally regarded as a trespasser and action can be started to eject the tenant.

tenancy by the entirety—a form of joint tenancy for husband and wife in some states. Neither spouse can separately convey the property.

tenancy in common—an undivided ownership by two or more joint owners. Upon the death of any owner his or her interest passes to the heirs.

termination statement—a statement filed to remove a personal property lien.

thin market—a market with very few buyers and sellers.

three-day notice—a notice given in many states to a tenant to quit or pay rent.

time is of the essence—a statement in an offer or option that acceptance must be made by a stated date or the right terminates.

time-share ownership—a joint ownership whereby various owners own block of time for which they have exclusive possession of the same property.

townhouse—usually a two-story residential unit with side walls common with other units.

township—an area six miles square containing thirty-six square miles. It is formed by government survey.

trade fixture—personal property installed by a tenant. Regardless of method of attachment, the tenant can remove the trade fixture prior to the end of the lease. The tenant must, however, repair damage caused by the removal.

trading on equity—borrowing money on equity in a property to invest in another property so that a greater return will be realized.

trust deed—a financing arrangement for real property in which the borrower (trustor) gives a note to a lender (beneficiary) and the title (trust deed) to a trustee to hold as security.

trustee—the third party to a trust deed who holds the trust deed.

trustor—the buyer or borrower under a trust deed.

unincorporated association—a nonprofit group. Title to property must be taken in individual members' names.

unit-in-place method—a method to determine replacement costs based on units such as a price per motel room or per electrical outlet.

unlawful detainer—the actual court eviction proceeding.

variable expenses—expenses of a business or investment which can be adjusted or deferred as opposed to fixed expenses such as taxes.

variance—an exception to zoning.

vendee—buyer.

vendor—seller.

walkup—a multistory apartment building without an elevator.

wrap-around loan—also known as an all-inclusive loan. A new mortgage, the wrap-around loan, is written for the amount of the first mortgage and the seller's equity. The seller collects on the wrap-around loan and then makes the payments on the first mortgage.

zoning—public restriction on use.

Index

Second mortgages, 31, 41, 43–44
Secondary financing, 36–37
Security deposits, 46, 89, 128
Self-analysis, 164–72
Seller's market, 78–79
Selling property, 151–63
Shape of parcel, 66
Single-family homes, 8–11, 56
Slum properties, 12, 55, 135
Society of Exchange Counselors, 112
Society of Real Estate Appraisers, 74
Special assessments, 89
Special purpose structures, 70
Stock cooperatives, 99–100
Straight line depreciation, 25
Straight loans, 37–38
Student housing, 125
Subdivisions, 95–105
Subject to a loan, 31, 91
Subletting, 147–48
Subordination, 42–43
Sum-of-the-years depreciation, 27
Swing loan, 39
Syndicates, 50–51

Tax sales, 58
Taxes, 1–2, 4–5, 18–28, 45–46, 100, 106–07, 152
Tenant relations, 130–31
Tenant selection, 135, 143–45
Tenants, 73
Termites, 72, 116
Timber, 124
Time shares, 102
Title insurance, 31, 90–91
Trading on equity, 39–40
Traffic, 66
Trust deeds, 30

Utilities, 64, 67, 137

VA loans, 8, 37
Vacancies, 13, 15, 68, 137–39
Vacation homes, 10–11
Value, 60–76, 81, 152–53
Variable rate mortgage, 38

Warehouses, 125–26
Wholesaling, 98
Wrap-around loan, 34

Zoning, 16–17, 62–63